Harris Rogers Schenck, Falling Spring Presbyterian Church

Proceedings at the Celebration

of the one hundred and sixtieth anniversary of the Falling Spring Presbyterian

Church, and the one hundredth anniversary of its existence as a separate charge,

November 10th, 11th, 12th and 14th, 1894

Harris Rogers Schenck, Falling Spring Presbyterian Church

Proceedings at the Celebration
of the one hundred and sixtieth anniversary of the Falling Spring Presbyterian Church, and the one hundredth anniversary of its existence as a separate charge, November 10th, 11th, 12th and 14th, 1894

ISBN/EAN: 9783337259990

Printed in Europe, USA, Canada, Australia, Japan

Cover: Foto ©Lupo / pixelio.de

More available books at **www.hansebooks.com**

1734   1794   1894

PROCEEDINGS

AT THE

CELEBRATION

OF THE

ONE HUNDRED AND SIXTIETH ANNIVERSARY

OF THE

Falling Spring Presbyterian Church,

AND THE

ONE HUNDREDTH ANNIVERSARY

OF ITS EXISTENCE AS A SEPARATE CHARGE;

November 10th, 11th, 12th and 14th, 1894.

HARRIS R. SCHENCK, Editor.

CHAMBERSBURG, PA.:
THE REPOSITORY PRESS.
1894.

TABLE OF CONTENTS.

	Page.
Cut of the Church of To-day,	Frontispiece.
Preface,	5
Preliminary Work,	7
Order of Services,	9
Dr. Niccolls' Address: Church and Home One Hundred Years Ago,	13
J. W. Sharpe's Address of Welcome,	34
Dr. Crawford's Historical Sermon,	36
Dr. Hibben's Paper,	53
Dr. Crawford's Personal Reminiscences,	57
Dr. Niccolls' Personal Reminiscences,	61
Mr. Schenck's Paper: Personal History of the Pastors,	
I. Rev. Samuel Caven, 1739-1741,	63
II. Rev. James Lang, 1767-1793,	67
III. Rev. William Speer, 1794-1797,	70
IV. Rev. David Denny, 1800-1838,	76
V. Rev. William Adam, 1840-1841,	82
VI. Rev. Daniel McKinley, D. D., 1841-1850,	89
VII. Rev. Joseph Clark, 1852-1857,	96
VIII. Rev. Lambert Suydam Fine, 1858-1859,	102
IX. Rev. Samuel Jack Niccolls, D. D., 1860-1864,	04
X. Rev. Joshua Blackwood Howell Janeway, Ph. D., 1866,	105
XI. Rev. John Agnew Crawford, D. D., 1867-1887,	107
XII. Rev. John Grier Hibben, Ph. D., 1887-1891,	111
XIII. Rev. Harris Rogers Schenck, 1892-	117
Mr. Bell's Paper: Greeting from the Greencastle Church,	118
Mr. Mackey's Paper: Greeting from the Central Church,	119
Dr. Platt's Paper: History of the Session,	121
The Charter,—(For the Deed, see page 39,)	129
Mr. McDowell's Paper: The History of the Trustees,	136
Mr. McIlvaine's Paper: Sketch of the Sabbath Schools,	148
Mrs. Reed's Paper: History of the Missionary Societies,	152
Mr. Reed's Paper: History of the Christian Endeavor Society,	158
The Officers of the Church, of the Congregation, and of the Societies,	161
Form of Reception of Members,	163
Extracts from the Presbyterian Standards, as to the Church and its Members,	168
Roll of Communicants,	172
Membership each year since April 1, 1822,	182
The Baptized Members and their relations to the Church,	183
Roll of Baptized Members,	189
Closing Words, by the Editor,	191

PREFACE.

As a true man loves his home, and a true patriot his country, so a true Christian loves his Church. Home and country and Church are the Christian's dearest earthly inheritances. Neither pride of ancestry, nor idolatry of stone and mortar, can be mistaken for genuine fruit-bearing love of Zion's "towers and bulwarks and palaces." (Ps. 48:12-13.) "A people who take no pride," says Macaulay, "in remembering and recording the deeds of their forefathers, will not be likely to do anything worthy to be remembered or preserved by posterity." And a godly ancestry is more to be desired than a great or wealthy. Thomas Guthrie once wrote, "Through my ancestry, as far as I can trace them, I can claim to be the seed of the righteous, a higher honor than the blue blood of which some boast." And Wm. Cowper well sang:

> "My boast is not that I deduce my birth
> From loins enthroned, and rulers of the earth;
> But higher far my proud pretensions rise,
> The son of parents passed into the skies."

The chief value of a study of the past is that we are thereby incited to the work of improving upon that past. It behooves the children of godly men to pass on to their children's children a record in which the latter shall rejoice as fully we rejoice in what is "the past" to us. No better prayer can be offered than this:

> "God of our fathers! be the God
> Of their succeeding race."

The authors of the addresses contained in this volume will feel that their efforts have not been in vain, if the youth of today shall be stirred to still better, nobler lives and deeds.

So far as possible, the proof-sheets have been read by the respective authors.

The editing of the volume has been a labor of love by one who counts it an honor to be a loyal son of the Presbyterian Church, and a joy as well to be the minister of "The Falling Spring Presbyterian Congregation."

H. R. S.

PRELIMINARY WORK.

At the monthly meeting of the Session of the Falling Spring Presbyterian Church, held at the Manse, June 4, 1894, attention was called to the fact that just one hundred years ago this church was separated from the Lower East Conococheague Church at Greencastle, and from that date has had an independent history. In view of this fact, the Session unanimously appointed the Pastor and Elder Platt a Committee to consider the advisability of celebrating this centennial. This Committee reported to the Session at its meeting, July 2, 1894, recommending that such a celebration be held, with some suggestions as to the programme. The Session thereupon unanimously adopted the recommendations, and approved of the provisional programme. On August 6, 1894, the Session enlarged the Committee by the addition of Elder W. G. Reed, and gave the said Committee full power to make all further arrangements. (Later on, the Pastor and Elder H. A. Riddle were made a Committee on Publication.)

At the request of the Committee, a joint meeting of the Session and Board of Trustees was held at the house of Mr. T. B. Kennedy. There were present : Harris R. Schenck, Pastor; Geo. F. Platt, Wm. B. Reed, H. A. Riddle, Elders ; T. B. Kennedy, J. M. McDowell, John Stewart and Wm. B. Reed, Trustees, (the last named being also an Elder.) At this meeting the following Committees were appointed :

ON SOCIAL REUNION: Mrs. Rose Senseny, Mrs. A. N. Pomeroy, Mrs. A. Buchanan, Mrs. T. M. Nelson, Mrs. Wm. Kennedy.

On Music : H. A. Riddle.

On Subscriptions : J. M. McDowell, W. B. Reed.

These Committees worked throughout in close harmony with the Session's Committee, and to their indefatigable efforts and their united interest, the complete success of the celebration is due. To the members of the choir the heartiest praise is also due. The following were its members: Musical Director, H. A. Riddle ; Organist, Miss Anna W. Stewart ; Sopranos, Miss Mary Snider and Miss Sallie Nelson and Miss Mary Stewart ; Altos, Mrs. John S. Kennedy and Miss Elsie K. Stewart ; Tenors, H. A. Riddle and D. O. Gehr ; Basses, E. B. Wiestling and Walter Holler.

The Music Committee of the Young People's Society of Christian Endeavor, under the chairmanship of Miss Madge Nelson, also added to the pleasures of the occasion by a carefully prepared programme of sacred music on Sabbath evening.

The decorations both in the Church and Chapel were very elaborate and beautiful, thanks to the skill and taste of the Ladies Committee and the Flower Committee of the Y. P. S. C. E. and its chairman, Miss Elizabeth A. McKnight.

Some interesting relics were exhibited, including manuscript sermons of former Pastors, portraits of former Elders, hymn-books in use in the first years of the organization of the choir, about 1830, and in later years, and many other relics loaned for the occasion.

Portraits of all the former pastors except the Rev. Samuel Caven, the Rev. James Lang, and the Rev. William Adam were hung upon the walls of the Chapel as a permanent collection. Pictures of the Church as it was in 1803, 1850, 1857 and 1894, were also a part of this collection.

Thus the history of the past will be frequently brought to mind. May that history incite us to larger thought and life in the coming years.

ORDER OF SERVICES.

SATURDAY, NOVEMBER 10, 1894, 7:00 P. M.

Anthem—"Praise Ye the Father," - - *Gounod.*
Doxology.
Invocation, - - REV. HARRIS R. SCHENCK, 1892–
Scripture.
Prayer, - - REV. J. A. CRAWFORD, D. D., 1867–86.
Hymn—No. 575, I love thy Kingdom, Lord.
Address—"Church and Home One Hundred Years Ago,"
                REV. S. J. NICCOLLS, D. D., 1860–64.
Prayer, - - - - REV. HARRIS R. SCHENCK.
Hymn—No. 569, Oh where are Kings and Empires now?
Benediction. - - - REV. S. J. NICCOLLS, D. D.
  Social Reunion in the Chapel, from 8:00 to 10:00 P. M.
Words of Welcome, - - - J. W. SHARPE, ESQ.
Letters from Absent Friends.
Music.

COMMITTEE OF RECEPTION.

The Pastor and Mrs. H. R. Schenck,
Mrs. Jane K. Senseny, Mrs. T. B. Kennedy, Mrs. Jos. Clark, Mrs. M. C. Washington, Mrs. Ellen Culbertson, Mrs. Wm. McLellan, Mrs. J. F. Kennedy, Mrs. Abigail Chambers, Mrs. Benj. George, Mrs. Margaret King, Mrs. W. G. Reed, Miss Mary King, and Mrs. O. N. Lull and Mrs. J. W. Craig of the Central Presbyterian Church.

SABBATH, NOVEMBER 11, 1894, 11 A. M.

Anthem—"Gloria," - - - - - *Mozart.*
Prayer, REV. T. J. SHERRARD, Pastor Central Pres. Church.

Scripture, - - - - Rev H. R. Schenck.
Hymn—No. 373, Let Children hear the Mighty Deeds.
Offering. "O Saviour of the World," - - *Goss.*
Historical Sermon, - - Rev. J. A. Crawford, D. D.
Prayer, - - - - Rev. S. J. Niccolls, D. D.
Hymn—No. 435, Our God, Our Help in Ages Past.
Benediction, - - - Rev. J. A. Crawford, D. D.

3.30 P. M.

Hymn—No. 1, Ye Servants of God, your Master proclaim.
Scripture.
Prayer, - - - Rev. J. A. Crawford, D. D.
Hymn—No. 312, My Jesus, as Thou wilt.
Sermon, 2 Cor. 1:3-4, - - Rev. S. J. Niccolls, D. D.
Prayer, - - - - Rev. J. F. Kennedy, D. D.
Hymn—No. 474, Nearer, my God, to thee.
Benediction, - - - Rev. S. J. Niccolls, D. D.

6:00 P. M. IN THE CHAPEL.

SERVICE OF SONG AND PRAISE.

Young People's Society of Christian Endeavor, 1888.
Duet, Jesus, Lover of my Soul, - *F. Campana.*
    Miss S. J. Nelson and W. F. Holler.
Solo, Sun of my Soul, - - - - - *Wagner.*
    Miss Elsie K. Stewart.
Solo, Holy Father, Hear Us, - - - *M. F. Ludds.*
    Miss S. J. Nelson.
Solo, Ashamed of Jesus,
    Miss Grace Curriden.
Hymn, by the Society.
Solo, He giveth His Beloved Sleep, - - *Franz Abt.*
    W. F. Holler.
Hymn, by the Society.
Prayer, - - - - - - Rev. H. R. Schenck.

7:00 P. M.

Anthem—"Send out Thy Light," - - - *Gounod.*
Scripture, - - - - Rev. T. J. Sherrard.
Prayer, - - - - - Rev. H. R. Schenck.
Hymn—No. 964, The Church's One Foundation.
Offering. "Sweet is Thy Mercy," - - - *Barnby.*
Reminiscences, (paper read by H. A. Riddle)
      Rev. J. Grier Hibben, Ph. D.
Reminiscences, - - - Rev. J. A. Crawford, D. D.
Reminiscences, - - - Rev. S. J. Niccolls, D. D.
Hymn—No. 808, Holy Father! Thou hast Taught Us.
Prayer, - - - - - Rev. H. R. Schenck.
Hymn—No. 597, Blest Be the Tie that Binds.
Benedictus.

MONDAY, NOVEMBER 12, 1894, 7:00 P. M.

Anthem—"The King of Love my Shepherd is," *Gounod.*
Scripture.
Prayer, - Rev. Samuel McLanahan of Baltimore, Md.
Hymn—No. 570, O Lord of hosts! How lovely is, The
   Place where Thou Dost Dwell.
Paper—"The Personal History of Former Pastors,"
      Rev. Harris R. Schenck.
Hymn—No. 583, How Beauteous are their Feet.
Brief Addresses:
 On behalf of the Greencastle Church, (formerly Lower East
   Conococheague,) Rev. L. Carmon Bell, Pastor.
 On behalf of the Central Presbyterian Church, a child of
   this Church, 1868–1894. Elder W. H. H. Mackey.
Prayer,- - - - - - Rev T. J. Sherrard.
Doxology.
Benediction, - - - - Rev. H. R. Schenck.

WEDNESDAY, NOVEMBER 14, 1894, 7:30 P. M.

Hymn.
Scripture, - - - - Rev. H. R. Schenck.
Prayer, - - - - - Rev. T. J. Sherrard.
Brief Addresses :
On behalf of the Session, - Elder Platt, Clerk, 1864–
On behalf of the Trustees,
     J. M. McDowell, Secretary *pro tem*.
On behalf of the Sabbath School,
     J. S. McIlvaine, Assistant Superintendent.*
On behalf of the Missionary Societies and Bands,
     Mrs. W. B. Reed.
On behalf of the Y. P. S. C. E. - Mr. W. B. Reed.
Hymn.
Benediction, - - - Rev. J. A. Crawford, D. D.

---

*Mr. McIlvaine was unable to be present.

CHURCH AND HOME ONE HUNDRED YEARS AGO.

Beloved Brethren of the Falling Spring Church:

The unique occasion, which has called us together, has for me, a special interest. The history of this venerable church holds a period of my life which I can never forget. It so happens that I am one of the links in a chain, which binds the events of a remote past to this present.

It is my happy lot to be one in the line of pastors who ministered to this church since its independent life, one hundred years ago. I regard it as an honor, and a privilege, to have a place in such an apostolic succession. No happier years of life have ever come to me than those which I spent here, with the people of my first love, to whom my heart still clings with undying affection. The dreams of night have often carried me back to these scenes of my earliest labors in the gospel ministry, and in them I have again become your pastor, and have heard the familiar voices, and seen the dear faces of those who more than a quarter of a century ago, gave me their confidence and their love.

As I now look upon these familiar surroundings, the venerable church, the rushing waters of Falling Spring, and the green God's Acre, in which slumber in peace so many that are dear to us,—memories are awakened that carry me away as with a flood. This present scene grows dim and shadowy, and behind it in colors of life I see the past. There come before me the grey haired fathers, the men and women, the boys and girls, of thirty years ago. What a goodly company! My heart leaps to be among them; they lived in no common years, for the atmosphere then was electric, and the days big with destiny for our country, and for the race. Some of them still remain, but transformed ; black locks have whitened, and once erect forms bend under the burden of years. Ruddy-faced youths have become stalwart men ; and sweet-faced, laughing girls are stately matrons. But the majority have passed to that land from which no answer comes, either to our entreaties or to our sobs. Sweet is their memory, and blessed the ministry of their lives!

But I must not linger upon that which lies within the compass of my memory. The event which we commemorate demands a wider range of thought. It is wise for us to reflect upon the past, and to mark those springs of influence whose streams water and make glad the present. There is no such things as isolation in human affairs. Human life is a continuous stream, and we can no more escape the past than we can the future. We build upon what the fathers have done. We are rich or poor according to the legacies they have left us ; but alas ! we are not always wise in our valuation of what we have inherited, and we barter priceless heirlooms for new fashioned and tawdry ornaments of little worth.

My theme takes us out of this noisy, bustling and boasting 19th century, to the close of the 18th. It is difficult to realize what the backward stride of a century means. It takes us to a period when all the great inventions, which have had so much to do with human progress and civilization during the present century, were unknown. Railroads and telegraphs and telephones were not even dreamed of. Roads were few and poor, and the means of travel rude and primitive. Intercourse between different parts of the country was difficult, and each community lived by itself. The first steamboat did not move on American waters until 1807, nor

had the now obsolete stage-coach begun its course across the
mountains. The homes of one hundred years ago, in this
fair valley, had little of what we call the comforts of life.
Matches had not yet taken the place of the tinder box, nor
stoves supplanted the huge open fire-places. There were
still in use the primitive methods of spinning and weaving;
good wives, like Solomon's virtuous woman, laid their hands
to the distaff, and men were content to wear suits of homespun. Silks and broadcloths were the rare badges of wealth.
The transformation of the primitive log houses into buildings of stone and brick, had just commenced. The prime-
val forests, from which the savage Indians had only recently
been driven, still stood in their native grandeur and beauty,
their edges rent and torn with "clearings," which heralded
the incessant war which was being waged for their destruc-
tion: the streams swarming with fish, and the thickets with
game, made a hunters' paradise. It was in short, a community laying the foundations of a new civilization. The
larger world, to which the inhabitants of this valley were
related, was then slowly emerging from the shadows of the
middle ages. 1794 was the time of the Reign of Terror in
France, and the effects of that wild, mad, and titanic struggle for liberty on the part of a brave people were being felt
throughout the civilized world. In England, George III,
insane by turns, was on the throne, and the great statesmen,
Pitt and Fox and Burke, were moving the pieces on the
chess-board of the nations. In our own country the revered
Washington was president, serving his second term; the
Republic, dating its organization from the inauguration of
its first president, was only five years old. Adams, Jefferson
and Franklin were alive. Such princes in the world of
letters as Gibbon, Voltaire, Cowper and Burns, had either
just passed away, or were still lingering in the weakness of
old age. It was no time of quiet. The great nations of

Europe were at war with each other. New ideas, which since then have embodied themselves into new states, laws and customs, were abroad among the people fermenting and begetting revolutions. The signs of the times indicated that great changes were at hand, and men then, looked to the incoming 19th century with as much interest and hope as we do to the 20th, now at hand. It is under such circumstances and in such relations, that we find our ancestors, one hundred years ago. They, or their fathers, had come to this fairest valley of the new world, to find homes for themselves. They were not like our modern emigrants, searchers after gold, or speculators in land; they came with their wives and children to plant the family; and while with their ideas of thrift, they were not indifferent to fortune, their first care was to use the axe and plow to secure the welfare of home.

The conditions of society then were such as to intensify the life of home. The members of the family were mutually dependent on each other; not only common blood, but common toil and common purposes bound them together. Channels of trade and commerce were not open to any great extent, in a valley so remote from the seaboard as this. There were no large factories, or shops, or houses of trade, to furnish employment and attract the youth from home. The great revolution in society, so portentous and far-reaching in its effects, which modern machinery has made in the 19th century, had not as yet begun. The chief industries were home industries. The chief market was that of home; each family raised its own flax and wool, and spun the yarn and wove its own garments. Each had its own flocks and herds; each was its own butcher and baker; from their own fields they gathered the grain or corn; their horses carried to the nearest mill and back again what was needed for meal or flour, and the surplus found transformation into an acceptable and potable form in the family still-house. There was little need for money; the exchange of commodities between families was all that was required; home was supreme as the centre of trade and manufacture. No great cities with their strong attractions for gain, drew the young men and maidens away from the shelter of the paternal roof; at most, they went out a little way in the neighborhood to learn a trade, apprenticed to some well known mechanic. And when mating-time came, like bees swarming from the hives, they went out to build another home close by.

Home also, dominated the social life of the community in a way greatly different from its power at the present day. The mutual dependence of families developed a kind of hospitality which is almost unknown in our modern life. Very few in these days would dare to come, accompanied with their families, to spend not simply an evening, but a night or even several days with their neighbors; or to so time their visit as to be sure that they would be present at meal-times; yet such was the general custom one hundred years ago. My lady rushing about, card case in hand and making a brief call of ten minutes, would have been regarded as a semi-lunatic, or at least as one of "the foolish women," possessed by some foreign ideas. The free, open and hearty hospitality of these early homes was one of their distinguishing characteristics. The passing traveler found a ready welcome, and free entertainment for man and beast. Social life, as it centered in the home, had its attractive features. Let no one suppose that those days of strict principles, rigid rules, catechisms, long sermons, and careful Sabbath observances, were joyless ones in the family. Their social gatherings, while they may have lacked what we call refinement and polish, were not inferior to any modern ones in cheerful entertainment, innocent mirth and true sociability.

I do not refer to the "log-rollings," "huskings," or muster-days, the times of coarse frolicking, when drunkenness and fighting were not uncommon, and Scotch-Irish pugnacity manifested itself in many unseemly ways; but rather to the friendly gatherings of the neighbors in each others houses. It is not difficult to imagine one of these evenings at home. The family is gathered around the open fireplace, in which the burning logs crackle and spark as with sympathetic joy. The ruddy flame roars up the black-throated chimney, and the shadows dance and chase each other over the well-swept and uncarpeted floor. Suddenly, footsteps and a loud knocking, announce the coming of visitors, and the circle around the fire is enlarged to give them a place in the genial heat and light. Another, and another come; fathers and mothers arrive bringing the young folks, and the circle grows wider; another log is added to the fire, and its flames dance and leap more merrily. The men talk, as men do now, of the news of the day, mainly neighborhood matters; the women of household affairs, and the children drawn together by the sweet freemasonry of childhood, start their games, or listen breathlessy to the oft-told stories of some old soldier of the war of Independence, or of a bold Indian fighter and his hair-breadth escape from savage foes. There is no restraint or formality. There are jokes, and repartee, and laughter, not nicely modulated, but hearty and loud. The good wife at last brings out from the household store the refreshment for her guests; hickory-nuts and walnuts, apples, pies and cakes; for drink there is cider, nor do the men fail to take that which every well furnished house contained, whiskey, judged necessary to keep out the cold in winter, as well as the heat in summer. They return early, and ten o'clock finds all in bed, and the fire on the hearth slumbering quietly under its blanket of ashes.

A short time ago in a home west of the Mississippi, I

came across a volume in which were some old letters written by a Chambersburg girl, which gave some interesting glimpses into the home life of one hundred years ago. One dated Chambersburg, December 17th, 1793, addressed to her mother, reads;

"Last Saturday we set out in a sleigh, amidst a volley of snowballs sent after us by Mr. Dunlop, to visit Dr. and Mrs. Johnson. For several miles no persons were ever better pleased with themselves and each other. Nature smiled in her white vestments, pure as innocence and peaceful as ourselves; but alas! a fateful stump, as if to teach us the mutability of human happiness, proved fatal to our progress; in an instant we were all thrown out and enveloped in snowdrifts. One part of the sleigh remained with us; the other attached to the horses was proceeding to the Doctor's as though the Furies were driving. Mr. Calhoun set off as soon as he could disengaged himself to overtake them, and if possible be in at the "brush." It would have been a severe "brush" to us, but for a little one horse sleigh, that but a few moments before had afforded us a subject for the greatest merriment. After a hearty laugh at our expense, its owner took us in and conveyed us to our destination."

The winter, then, because of enforced cessation from toil in the fields, was specially the time for social enjoyment, but it was not by any means a time of idleness. The loom and spinning wheel were busy, and varied domestic duties gave ample employment for the household. Summer brought its toil in planting and reaping, but it was still family work, in which all had a share.

It was in the main, home life among agricultural people, a life of simplicity, frugality and honest toil; but we would sadly misconceive it, if we supposed it, a hard and joyless one. If those early homes had less of what we call the adornments and the comforts of life, it is certain they had as much, if not more, of true happiness; for that does not depend upon carpeted floors, costly furniture and the upholsterers' art. Those who have reached ease and plenty through toil and self-denial, can testify that some of their happiest days were those of their earlier years, when they were struggling in hope of something better, and found a sweet content in their little gains.

Happiness can sit at the humble fireside, clad in homespun garments, and be as truly herself, as when robed in silks, adorned with jewels, and dwelling in a palace: nay, oftener does she come with her smiling face to the lowly home where honest thrift, daily toil, and united aims bind the household together.

The pride of fathers and the joy of mothers in their children were just as great a hundred years ago as now; the wine of life was then as intoxicating to youth, and young maidens knew as much of the sweetness of love, when to the merry hum of the spinning wheel, they listened to their lovers' tender words, as do the modern ones resting on damask cushions, and hearing the sweet old story, to the accompaniment of the piano.

Nor was home life then all Arcadian simplicity and unbroken content; alas, there is no happy valley on earth within whose compass men can find perfect peace, and satisfaction for all their aspirations. It could not be said of all who lived in this valley then, that;

. "Along the cool, sequestered vale of life,
They kept the noiseless tenor of their way,

There was then as now, a larger world beyond, whose influence was more or less felt, and whose charm fell on some with delight.

The letters to which I have already referred, give some glimpses of it. One, dated, Philadelphia, February 25th,

1795, gives us a description of the celebration of Washington's birthday, and of a reception to the President.

"The morning of the 22nd was ushered in by the discharge of heavy artillery. The whole city was in commotion, making arrangements to demonstrate their attachment to our beloved President. The Masonic, Cincinnati and the military orders united in doing him honor. Happy Republic, great and glorious!

"Mrs. Cadwaleder was too indisposed to attend the ball; Mr. and Mrs. Jackson with Dr. Spring called for me in their coach. Dr. Rodman met us at the door and conducted us to Mrs. Washington. She half arose as we made our passing compliments. She was dressed in a rich silk entirely without ornament, except the animation her amiable heart gave to her countenance. Next her were sitting the wives of foreign embassadors, glittering with ornaments from the floor to the summit of their head dress. One of the ladies wore three large ostrich feathers. Her brow was encircled by a sparkling fillet of diamonds. Her neck and arms were almost covered with jewels, and two watches were suspended from her girdle, all reflecting the light from a hundred directions. Such superabundance of ornaments struck me as injudicious. We look too much at the gold and pearls to do justice to the lady.

The seats were arranged like those of an amphitheatre, and cords were stretched on each side of the room about three feet from the floor, to preserve sufficient space for the dancers. We were not long seated when General Washington entered and bowed to the ladies, as he passed around the room. "He comes, he comes, the hero comes," I involuntarily and softly exclaimed. When he bowed to me, I could scarcely resist the impulse of my heart that almost burst through my bosom, to meet him. On this evening, my dress was white brocaded silk, trimmed with silver and white silk, high heel shoes embroidered with silver, and a light blue sash, with a silver cord and tassel tied at the left side. My watch was suspended at the right, and my hair was in its natural curls. Surmounting all, was a small white hat, and white ostrich feather confined by a brilliant pin and buckle."

But there is still another feature of the home life of our fathers, which must not be overlooked. It is its religiousness. Whatever we may think of the piety of that age, or whatever may have been its defects, it was profoundly serious and earnest. It made itself felt in all the regulations of home. It set up a family altar, with its morning and evening sacrifice of praise and prayer. It made the Bible the supreme law of the household, and men, to the best of their ability, set their consciences by it, as they did their clocks by the sun, deeming both infallible, in all their directions. In their simple faith, they looked upon children as gifts from God, the more the better, and they trained them in the nurture and admonition of the Lord. The admonition was at times made humanly severe and rigorous, but it was ever true to the end in view. Family government was not then in the hands of the children, but with the parents, according to God's Ordinance. The catechism had to be learned, nor was attendance upon the sanctuary an optional matter with the children. The infant in the mother's arms, and the eldest-born, reaching his majority, were alike brought to the Sabbath services. The family as a unit was expected to attend, nor was any day in the family life more marked than the Sabbath. Its sanctity was not to be violated by any needless work, nor by social visiting, nor by any loud speech or boisterous mirth. Whistling was an impropriety, and the playing of any musical instrument a serious offense. Even the preparation of food allowable on other days, or walking idly abroad, was forbidden. The playfulness of children was repressed, and an air of solemnity pervaded the house. The day stood alone, reminding them of the awful presence of the invisible God, and of their obligations to Him. It was one of the most important educators of home life, and it can easily be seen how it made a deep impression upon character. It is quite common to speak of the old-time Sabbath observances with a sneer, as a remnant of Jewish bondage, or as creating a distaste for religion. They have been described as sombre and awful days, lacking in the freeness and sweetness of the gospel dispensation. Some did feel them to be a restraint and a burden, but not all. There are those to whom, in after years, their memory was a delight. Let our young lady from Chambersburg testify on this point. This is what she writes in the year 1818: "Oh, that we could rightly estimate the privilege of having one-seventh of our time secluded from the busy world. I yet recollect a Sabbath evening walk at Loudoun. The day had passed in retirement and useful reading and conversation, when our mother proposed a walk to the hills. Bella and I accompanied her, and we pursued a path through a meadow, around a gentle hill, and crossed a stile, coming to a forest. Here we paused. On the opposite side of the meadow was a broad creek not disturbed as on other days, by the wheels of different mills, reflecting on its smooth, clear surface the luxuriance of its bank. All nature seemed to enjoy its Sabbath; all was still. The distant houses in view were closed, the cattle grazed undisturbed, and Mount Parnell's summit received the brilliant rays of the declining sun. Our dear mother, aware of the importance of early religious impressions, said to us: 'How sublime will be an eternal Sabbath.' The stillness of the air, the grandeur of the trees, the notes of the evening bird, and the conversation with our mother, occasioned an unusual seriousness. She spoke of the evil propensities of the heart, the necessity of virtuous principle, the importance of revelation as an infallible guide, assuring us that no mere personal advantage could secure our happiness. 'It is' said she 'the religion of Jesus alone that can give peace and eternal felicity.' Then kneeling, with one of us on each side of her, she prayed. I look upon this as the most sublime moment of my life. I felt myself introduced to God."

Certain it is that out of such homes, and from such training, came men and women who felt as none other, their obligations to God. Their religious convictions were clear and strong. Life to them was a serious affair; but there was a high and solemn gladness in it, like the joy of angels, for they felt that in all its conflict, sorrows and temptations, they were serving God, and could have His smile of approval.

Their moral opinions were as stalwart as their bodies. It may have been Spartan discipline that they received, but it made heroes. There is no factor more potent in society for good or ill, than home life. It is the fountain head of both Church and State, and gives character to each of them. It is not too much to say that the old, God-fearing homes of the Cumberland Valley have affected most powerfully the civilization of our country. Their descendants, multiplied into millions, still feel and perpetuate the pious influences of their ancestral home.

The other part of my theme relates to the Church. The religious beliefs of a people are the supreme forces in developing their social and national life. They ultimately modify and control laws, customs, education, in short all that enters into their civilization. According as their beliefs are pure and true, or corrupt and superstitious, the people rise or fall in the scale of nations. It is a well known fact that the early settlers of this valley were almost exclusively Scotch-Irish, and Presbyterians in their faith. They heartily accepted the Westminster symbols in their entirety, and believed that they had the only true, scriptural polity of Church government. Their ancestors had held the same faith, and so it was in their blood. It had been received as a priceless heirloom from men who had fought for it, and suffered and died for it. It was the faith of martyrs and confessors, of whom the world was not worthy. They hated the papacy as the embodiment of anti-Christ, a cruel persecutor, drunk with the blood of saints. They hated Episcopacy with only a less hatred, because it resembled "the scarlet woman," and it too had been their persecutor. They were not exempt from intolerance, sectarianism and bigotry, judged by our times; but they were tolerant of the faith of others, judged by their own times. That is to say, they did not persecute others by force for their religious opinions, although they had the power to do it; they suffered the Quakers and the Mennonites to remain unmolested in their midst. They did not maltreat the Methodists when they appeared, but they did look upon them as a poor, benighted people, led astray by religious fanaticism and more worthy of pity or contempt than respect. Their ecclesiastical relations with others were like those of the ancient Jews and Samaritans. But whatever may have been their defects in Christian love, and they were those of their time, there can be no doubt that they held a faith which wrought most powerfully for righteousness in human society. The undiluted Calvinism which was preached to them, and on which they fed with relish, could not but prove a mighty incentive to right moral action. It not only quickened the mind by bringing before it the most stupendous abstract questions that could occupy its attentions, but it gave to those questions an awful reality, and a direct application to human life. Its central doctrine was the sovereignty of God, to which all must bow in unquestioning submission. It looked upon all men as ruined and lost under the power of sin, and none might hope for salvation save through the operations of sovereign grace, saving according to its own good pleasure. But this doctrine was not preached or held as a grim fatalism, manifesting itself in arbitrary decrees which bound men as in chains; on the contrary, it was insisted that the soul of man was ever free, that he was always responsible for his actions, that in accordance with the divine commands and promises, this saving and sovereign grace was to be sought after, and that its reception meant perserverance in righteousness. It was a faith that inspired and compelled action. The men of that day believed strenuously, not in man's fore-ordination, but in God's; so their chief care was to hold themselves in harmony with His decrees. This gave a strength and boldness to their convictions which nothing could crush. They did not change their characters or their conduct with their circumstances. They would do on earth, that which would pass inspection at the Supreme Court in Heaven. The sense of duty grew strong, rugged and unyielding as iron, in the light of the doctrine of divine sovereignty, as revealed in the written Word. While it set their consciences free from all the commandments and traditions of men, it also made them uncompromising in following what they believed to be the teachings of Holy Scripture. They were an impractical sort of people to those who wished to guide conduct by expediency, or gain peace by compromise.

Perhaps they were sometimes over-scrupulous, and did not always distinguish between their prejudices and their consciences. Admit that they were at times angular and exacting; but it was by such men that the foundations of a great republic were laid, and who will find fault with the granite block because its corners are not smooth as silk, and soft as wool?

This same Calvinistic faith developed within them, as it has done everywhere, the possibilities of self government. It made the atmosphere most favorable for true freedom. The men whose consciences would not permit them to kneel to any object or being, other than the living and invisible God, were already free men and fit for a free government. So it was when on the 4th of July, 1776, the Liberty Bell in Phildelphia rang out the tidings that the colonies had declared their independence, in this valley the hearts of the people responded in joy as the heart of one man. Nowhere did patriotic fervor burn higher or more brightly than among the Presbyterian Scotch-Irish. From this very place a company marched to Boston and took part in the famous struggle on Bunker Hill; and it was in this very Church that an attempt was made, through excessive zeal, to discipline a member because it was suspected that his sympathies were not wholly with the patriotic cause.

The teaching from the pulpit one hundred years ago, while evangelical, was strongly doctrinal in its character. Special emphasis was given to the distinctive features of Calvinism, and its famous five points of doctrine found long elucidations and fervent applications. The instruction given was systematic, and in a direct line with the doctrinal teachings of the Westminster catechisms, and as a result, the people knew what they believed. There were also systematic expositions of Scripture, generally a series of discourses on particular books of the sacred volume; a kind of expository preaching which has fallen largely into disuse at the present time. Nor were the church-goers of those days afraid of a long sermon. They expected an hour, or even more, to be spent in opening up the Word. They cared not so much for exhortation as for solid instruction, and they got it. They wanted strong meat; not milk for babes. There was also a stern simplicity in the manner of worship, which was strikingly in accord with their faith. A century nearer to reformation struggles than we are, they had an intense aversion to anything like forms, ceremonials, rituals or even decorations in the church. All these seemed to them to savor of popery. It was something that tended to obscure, rather than reveal spiritual things. Their houses of worship were severely plain and unadorned. Stained glass, especially if marked by some sacred symbol, or even by the sign of the cross, would not have been tolerated. Organs would not have been allowed in the service of praise. The psalmody used was the old rugged Rouse's version. The singing of hymns was objected to as the offering of strange fire upon the altar. The communion was celebrated at long intervals, and was introduced by a fast day, and special services. The communicants partook of it seated at a table, and it was necessary to receive a token from the elders in order to participate in it. At that time there was no little complaint upon the part of some pious souls, of formalism and coldness in the church. The weekly prayer meeting had not as yet become the custom, nor was the Sunday school in existence. Years ago it was my privilege to read the manuscript containing the constitution and rules of the first Sunday school organized in this church. Its accounts were kept in pounds, shillings and pence. Each Sabbath there was a new superintendent, and the instruction consisted largely in reciting the catechism, and repeating portions of the Scriptures. The churches, especially in the new settlements, were struggling for existence, and there was not as yet any foreign missionary spirit among them. The times of refreshing from the Lord had not yet come. The General Assembly of 1799 "laments the declination of the vital spirit of religion and the abundance and boldness of impiety and immorality;" it said: "a vain and pernicious philosophy has in many instances spread its infection over Europe and

America, and the introduction of a multitude of licentious and unprincipled writings have poisoned the source of morals in certain classes of society, or in particular districts of the church." It called earnestly upon its ministers to exert themselves to resist the progress of vice and profaneness, and to advance the principles and practice of virtue and piety. Drunkenness was the prevailing vice of the time, greatly fostered by social customs, and the prevailing type of unbelief was of the gross, ribald school of Tom Paine. The Presbyterian ministers of that period were unquestionably the foremost in influence, scholarship and general culture. They were for the most part liberally educated, and they became the leading teachers as well as preachers in the community. True to the genius of Presbyterianism, they were strenuous advocates of popular education, and the academies and colleges of that period were in the majority of cases, organized and established through their instrumentality. The pastor of this church one hundred years ago, Rev. William Speer, was a fair representative of the ministry of that day. His piety was ardent and self denying, and his preaching solemn and practical. His zeal in the missionary cause led him to resign his charge after three years' service and go to Chillicothe, then in the territory of the Northwest. Subsequently, on account of domestic affliction, he returned to Western Pennsylvania and became the pastor of the churches of Greensburg and Unity. One of these churches I attended in my boyhood, and the memory of this godly man was still cherished in the traditions of the people. After him, in the year 1800 came the Rev. David Denny, who remained in this pastorate for 38 years. When I came among you in 1860, there were those living who had enjoyed his ministrations, and who held him in affectionate remembrance. He was a type of another class in the ministry of that period. He was not a brilliant orator, but his fidelity as a pastor, and the manifest sincerity of his Christian character gave more than the power of eloquence to his discourses, which were plain, systematic and direct presentations of the gospel. He wore well, and enjoyed in a more than ordinary degree, the esteem and affection of the whole community. In addition to his pastoral labors, he taught in the academy which still exists among you.

Time fails me, nor does it fall within the limits of my subject to speak of his successors. One of them was Rev. Daniel McKinley, D. D., who preached and labored with the zeal of an apostle, and who was known in all the churches for his consecration and his success in his Master's service. Another was Rev. Joseph Clark, able and scholarly, who labored here with great acceptance until 1859, when he resigned his church on account of failing health.

We have taken but a brief glance at the state of affairs in the church 100 years ago. We have seen earnest and heroic men and women toiling in building up the kingdom of Christ. Their work at best was incomplete and imperfect. "Through the ages one increasing purpose runs," and the best any generation can do, is to hasten the fulfillment of that purpose a little by its toil, and to leave an unfinished work to its successor. But the completion is sure to come, and the day will dawn when the top stone shall be laid with shoutings of "Grace, grace unto it."

Within the limits of a century there is room for advance and we ought to notice some progress. In some things we are better than our fathers. At least we have some better things granted to us, for which we must thank God. There has been a change in theology, not in its great essential doctrines, but in their perspective and arrangement. It has become more Christo--centric. Less emphasis is placed upon distinctive doctrine, and more upon the person of Christ. There is less of denominational zeal and more of missionary fervor. The fires of ecclesiastical controversy that once burned so fiercely, have largely died out. There is less importance attached to different shades of doctrinal opinion, and more to the direct application of the gospel to the needs of man. Christianity has become more genial and sympathetic, and concerns itself more about the sorrows and sufferings of man in this life. The church has awakened more fully to her missionary service, and feels as never before her obligations to preach the gospel to the whole world. The air at the close of the 19th century is not that of the close of the 18th. There is more of the subtle power of spring, more warmth and sunshine in it; the light of a brighter hope shines on us.

But if there is gain, there may also be loss. All forward movement is not progress. The age of which I speak had its defects, but so has our own, and if increasing light makes greater responsibility, our defects are the more serious. If our fathers emphasized in excess the divine sovereignty in their theology, their view at least made them strong men, with inflexible principles. If they insisted strenuously upon the teachings of sound doctrine and were intolerant of any deflection from orthodoxy, they had at least clear and positive convictions of truth, and were not driven to and fro by every idle gust of opinion. However it might be with others, they never lost sight of the deep and eternal distinction between right and wrong. If, as charged, they were at times narrow and intolerant in their opinions, those opinions had depth and strength and made their lives serious, dignified and forceful. If they were rough and angular, they were at least granite like men, fit to be the foundations to support the mighty superstructure that was to the reared on their achievements; what they were in faith and endurance made possible the better days to come. It is to be feared that we have lost some of the qualities that made them great and strong. If we are more liberal and tolerant in our views of doctrine, there is danger that they will degenerate into indifference to error. Insistence upon the divine love as the central fact in theology may lead us to forget the divine justice, and the holy demands of inexorable law. A revolt against doctrinal preaching may lead to the obscuring of the great essential facts of redemption, and the preaching of what is called a simple gospel, be nothing more than the proclamation of vapory sentiments which have no power to save men. We are in danger of exalting our boasted liberalism over the authority of the Word of God, and of making the gospel a means of securing prosperous living in this world, rather than eternal life in the world to come.

A revival of the spirit of our fathers in their uncompromising loyalty to Christ and His church, would not hurt, but rather help us. It would lead to a sharper separation between the church and the world, the better observance of the Lord's day, a higher standard of morals, a truer valuation of sound doctrine, and to clearer testimony for the truth.

There are also perils besetting us which did not face our fathers ; these grow out of the changed conditions of society ; out of increased luxury and the hurry and excitement of modern life. The old isolation which while it may have led to narrowness of thought, still intensified it, has gone. The general dissemination of education, and modern inventions have made us sharers in the life of the world. The thoughts of men, Christian and anti-Christian, the convictions and opinions of all lands are mingled in the intellectual and moral atmosphere which we breathe. The demands of modern life give us little time for discrimination, for meditation and devotion. We are in danger of being secularized and have already lost much of the intensity that characterized the piety of former days. The philosophic theology of the past never had an attitude so dangerous to our holy faith as modern speculative thought, or so-called criticism which would subvert the very foundations of revealed truth. The supernatural was not a matter of doubt to our fathers; now it is beset with doubt and assailed both in the name of science and rational religion.

We need to beware lest in our boasted progress we are only drifting away from our old secure anchorage and are being carried out into a sea of confusion and darkness. I rejoice to know that this grand old church remains true to its historic faith, and that same Gospel which strengthened and comforted our fathers is still faithfully preached to you.

ADDRESS OF WELCOME.

We have gathered here for the purpose of celebrating an anniversary, and the exercises of this evening are an introduction to the exercises that are to follow and be continued for several days. That the object of this anniversary had an honored existence is evidenced by the fact that we have gathered to celebrate it, as we are accustomed to celebrate only those lives or existences in which we can take a just pride and have a pleasure in recalling.

The subject of this celebration has had an honored existence, and we should come with joyous hearts, deeming it a privilege to participate in the exercises which commemorate the 160th anniversary of the founding of "The Falling Spring Church" and on the rounding of the full century mark as a separate and independent organization. When a man has lived a life that distinguishes him among his fellows and honors cluster around his head, the measure of whose days is full of deeds of loyal service and devotion to the cause of humanity, the day that brought him into this world is sometimes recognized and set apart for the purpose of extolling his virtues and singing his praises. When nations become great they glory, on stated occasions, to celebrate their prosperity. Those of us who attended the Columbian Exposition saw the United States celebrate the discovery of the continent of which it formed a part, on a scale of magnificence and grandeur, the like of which the world had never seen. And well it might so celebrate, for no celebration, however magnificent, could approach in grandeur the good that the land of the Stars and Stripes has conferred on man.

These are but human institutions, and if it is proper to

celebrate the day and year that gave them birth, how much more appropriate to recognize the time when a Divine Institution was given to the world.

It is the continued existence of such an institution that we are commemorating. More than a century and a half ago God planted his vineyard on this Hill. Generation after generation has passed away yet notwithstanding the changes of years and despite the ravages of death the light on this Zion's Hill has been steadily burning, revealing the cross pointing heavenward and proclaiming that Jesus Christ died to save sinners. And how the Lord has watered this vineyard and nurtured and blessed it; what precious fruit the vines have born and what rich vintage the Lord has gathered from time to time to himself.

But I must stop. It is not my province to lead you into this vineyard so full of historic interest—that field has been assigned to others.

We have with us those, who, in the years gone by, have had charge of this vineyard, labored in it and watered it with their prayers, and perhaps their tears. Tender memories still cling about their persons and with the feelings of affection and esteem strengthened by absence, on behalf of the flock they used to feed, I am to express to them the intense satisfaction and pleasure it gives their old congregation to again have them in their midst.

To them and to all those who have been identified in the past with The Falling Spring Church and are now with us, I extend a most cordial welcome. It is earnestly hoped that the years intervening since they left us will be blotted out and they will feel as though they were one of us again.

We trust that these anniversary exercises may increase our interest in and devotion to this dear old church, and quicken our zeal and love for the Lord who not only planted this vineyard but has continued it and blessed it so richly.

HISTORICAL SERMON.

DEUT. XXXII. 7, 9. "Remember the days of old, consider the years of many generations: ask thy father, and he will shew thee; thy elders, and they will tell thee. For the Lord's portion is his people; Jacob is the lot (cord) of his inheritance."

JOB VIII. 8-10. Inquire, I pray thee, of the former age, and prepare thyself to the search of their fathers: (for we are but of yesterday,) shall not they teach.

We turn to-day to front the Past, to look into a section of it which, for us as a congregation, has great attraction and significance. It would go ill with us, and with the whole church as well, were we shut away from the past, from God's great past, august, majestic as it is, and with the white of the eternities upon it.

Men think of it as perished utterly or as dim with the dust of the ages so that it cannot be seen, or as a buried thing with no possible resurrection.

But nothing is more real. Only it has register, and chronicle. Only it holds the lamps that do not go out, and the springs whose waters fail not. The present, to which we so strangely cling, and in which we think we live, is nought to the past, for what is it but the merest point, an unseen mystic pivot on which things revolve and by which they are turned over to the all engulfing past. What we think we have lost we shall find in it. And when we are in search of the realities, when we would know God, and find the mystic cross, and learn what is meant by the baptism of the Holy Ghost, or when we would see the cloven tongues of fire, we must needs go back into God's great Past. It only is historic: and not this alone but prophetic too, showing us the types and hints of that which is still to be.

We are here therefore to look into it, to listen to it. We are here to "ask of days that are past," to learn what we may of the Beginnings of our life and experiences as a church.

The history of our church is so woven with the history of our town that to give the one we must, to some extent, give also the other. In the year 1736 the region lying west of the Susquehanna was purchased of the Indians. As early indeed as 1682 grants had been made by Wm. Penn to parties in England, Ireland and Scotland, and in the following century numbers of these came over and settled in this region before the actual purchase of the land. Among them were four brothers by the name of Chambers who established themselves at Fishing Creek on the Susquehanna, in what is now Dauphin County, about 1726-7. They took up a large tract of land and built a mill. The Indians who were living in what is now the Cumberland Valley traded freely with them. Having learned from the Indians of the fertility and beauty of the particular section where our town now stands, two of the brothers, Benjamin and Joseph, came here; the latter returned presently to Fishing Creek, Benjamin remaining permanently. This was in the year 1730. Thos. Blunston, the agent of the "Proprietaries," gave to Benj. Chambers license to take up four hundred acres. He put up a log house near the spot where we now are, and gave the name of Falling Spring to the settlement, so-called because here the brook which now goes by that name falls into the creek. Buildings began to multiply, and in 1764 a town was laid out and named Chambersburg.

The settlers who had located along the waters of the Falling Spring were almost all Presbyterians. They were, therefore, not contented to remain long without the means of grace, and the established ordinances of the church. They were chiefly Scotch-Irish, and they showed the peculiar traits of that remarkable race, integrity, tenacity of purpose, high courage, intelligence, respect for law, self-respect, and above all a firm attachment to what they took to be the truth of God and the order of his house. With them the church was first, as you may suppose.

And therefore Col. Chambers very early set apart for church purposes, for a burial place, and for a school house, the acres here which are now the property of our congregation. In 1739, in the same year in which the Rev. Mr. Caven, the first pastor, was installed, there was put up a small log building which served for school purposes and for public worship. It was a plain structure, of course, with a door in the eastern side, and one in the southern. It was lighted, we are told, by long narrow windows the width of two small panes of glass, and reaching from one end of the building to the other. When the congregations were large the overflow was accommodated in a saw-mill which stood on what is now known as the island, where the Falling Spring enters the creek. This log building remained until about the year 1767, when one larger and of better material was put up. It was seventy feet long by thirty-five wide, and was replaced in 1803 by this stone building in which we worship now. This, as some of you will remember, had a small porch in front. During the pastorate of the Rev. Jos. Clark changes were made in the building. The porch disappeared, the vestibule was made part of the audience room, and the two towers were erected. Thus it remained until the year 1868 when, finding ourselves again in want of room, and wishing to improve still more the appearance of the house, the vestibule was removed, together, of course, with the small gallery at the eastern end. The front door was converted into a window, and the entrance was by the towers. The ceiling was made new. The present handsome pulpit and communion table—the gifts of Mr. and Mrs. T. B. Kennedy—were placed in the church, the stained glass was put in the windows, and the building took on the appearance which it has now. In 1876 the old stone wall which ran along the eastern edge of our church grounds was replaced by the present iron railing. This improvement, which is largely due to the energy of honorable women of the church, was made at a cost of about 1080 dollars. The stone steps at the gate were the gift of Miss Susan Chambers.

In 1768, just one year after the erection of the second building which,—as has been stated—took the place in 1767 of the original log building, Col. Benj. Chambers conveyed to the trustees these valuable and beautiful grounds. The deed runs thus :

"DEED for ground of Falling Spring Church, dated January 1, 1768 from Benj. Chambers, and Jane his wife, to Patrick Vance, Matthew Wilson, Edward Cook, Robt. Patterson, Wm. Lindsay, Jr., Wm. Goss, and Wm. Brotherton, in trust for the Presbyterian Congregation of Falling Spring now professing and adhering to, and that shall hereafter adhere to and profess the Westminster Confession of Faith, and the mode of Church Government therein contained ; witnesseth that the said B. Chambers, and Jane his wife, as well for their regard to the true religion of the blessed Redeemer Jesus Christ the Son of God, and for and in consideration of their regard to the interest and advantage of said congregation, and in consideration of the rents, convey to the trustees yielding and paying therefore and thereout unto the said B. Chambers, his heirs or assigns, at the said town of Chambersburg on the first day of June next first after this dates, the yearly rent or consideration of one Rose, if required."

This was duly attended to, as we learn, a rose being every year formally brought to Col. Chambers.

II.

I come now to speak of the organization of our church and to give such account as I can from the meagre material at command.

It is not possible to fix the date of its origin. The earlier minutes of the Donegal Presbytery, under whose care all the Presbyterians in the Valley originally were, make no record of the planting of any of the first churches. The calls given, and the pastoral relations constituted are recorded, but not the organization of the churches. We cannot therefore from any sources of information now open to us make sure of these distant dates.

The earliest reference which I have found in the minutes of Presbytery to our people in this part of the valley is in 1735, and the record is:

"April 4th, a supplication from the settlement over the river desiring supplies. The Presbytery appoints Mr. Alexander Craighead to supply said people the next two ensuing Sabbaths. Mr. Thompson also is appointed to supply at least two Sabbaths before the next meeting of Presbytery."

June 10, 1735. "Mr. Craighead and Thompson have supplied the people over the river as appointed." Whether this phrase, "the people over the river," applies to the Presbyterians of this section, or to those only who lived in what is now Cumberland County, I cannot determine. The presumption is that it includes them all.

The next reference in the Minutes to the people of this region is September 2d, 1736. "It being represented by Thos. Brown from Conococheague that Mr. Williams lately from England, who was rejected by our Presbytery, is likely to do harm to our interests by inveigling the people, Mr. Anderson is ordered to write to said people, and to dissuade them from entertaining him as a minister among them."

This shows that as early as 1736 and earlier indeed there must have been an organization here.

This Mr. Williams appears to have had no proper church relations, but to have been an adventurer whom our people, being much in need of supplies, engaged to preach to them. It would seem that the kindly remonstrance of the Presbytery had its effect, and they soon broke with Mr. Williams. At the same meeting, the Presbytery ordered a Mr. Golston who was to supply at Conodoguinet to preach here also. This was in September 1736. It must be remembered that at this time the name Conococheague, as it appears in the Minutes, included the churches of Chambersburg, Greencastle, Mercersburg, Loudon and the region round about.

I cannot determine precisely the year in which our church was first known by its present name. Probably it was in 1738 or 39, when—as we shall see—the people, without the sanction of Presbytery, divided the congregation into East and West Conococheague—the creek being the line of division. So that East Conococheague Church was made up of Falling Spring and Greencastle. There would seem to have been some difficulty before this time in regard to the boundary lines between our own congregation and other churches. For on August 31st, 1738 the record reads "Benj. Chambers moved to the Presbytery that the bounds be fixed between Hopewell—*i. e.*, Big Spring as now called—and upper Pennsboro, *i. e.*, Carlisle—and that commissioners be appointed from both places to attend at our next in order to a determination of the matter." And at the next meeting in October 28th, 1838 the record is:

"Robert Henry, a commissioner from Hopewell, complains

that the people of Falling Spring are about to encroach on Hopewell church. Ordered, that representatives from both attend our next, that the Presbytery may judge of said complaint." Mr. Craighead was afterwards appointed to visit these congregations and see what could be done.

It seems to me therefore perfectly fair to infer from all this history, and from the well-known attachment of these earliest settlers to their own church, and to its peculiar form of worship, also from the reference to the preaching of Mr. Williams in 1736, from the dispute as to the boundaries of Falling Spring and Big Spring which Col. Chambers referred to Presbytery in 1738—from all this it seems a fair inference that as early at least as 1734 or 1735 there was an organized congregation here. And we may, I think, take 1734 as the year of the birth of this church.

"At a meeting of Presbytery held at Pequa, Lancaster County, October 6, 1737, a young licentiate from the church of Ireland, Mr. Samuel Caven, appeared before the Presbytery, and having produced sufficient testimonials and preached to the satisfaction of the Presbytery, was received under its care." About a month later Mr. Samuel Thompson, also from Ireland, was received. It was "ordered that Mr. Thompson supply at Pennsboro, and Mr. Caven at Conococheague alternate months until our next." At the spring meeting, April 8th, 1738, held at Donegal, these young men reported that they had given the supplies. Pennsboro asked for the moderation of a call for Mr. Thompson; and Mr. Caven was sent again to supply Conococheague.

Of a meeting held at the Forks of Brandywine in June of the same year, 1738, the record reads thus : "Two supplications were presented to Presbytery by the people of Conococheague, viz: one by Benj. Chambers, desiring that a minister be appointed to moderate a call for Mr. Caven;

the other a supplication from Thos. Brown, desiring that a minister be sent to baptize children and to inspect the disorders of the congregation. Presbytery spent a pretty deal of time consulting as to these matters, and after all ordered Mr. Black to go upon this expedition about the beginning of August, and do what he can to answer the end of both supplications." Mr. Black fulfilled his appointment and this is the record on the books of Presbytery:

"August 31, 1738, Hanover. The affairs of Conococheague resumed, and several papers being read, and a pretty deal said by several persons on the affair, at last the Presbytery understanding that the people of the East and West side of the creek have agreed among themselves to divide into two societies, and that those on the East side have presented for Mr. Caven to be their minister, the Presbytery taking these things into consideration do, in the first place, considering the circumstances, approve of the division, though we think they have acted somewhat precipitately in separating without consent of Presbytery, and have likewise presented the call of the East side to Mr. Caven, which he has taken under consideration till our next." In the meantime he has to supply both East and West Conococheague.

At the meeting in October Mr. Caven asked to be excused until the next meeting from making answer to the call. Presbytery met again in December at Paxton, when he delivered a homily on Matthew v. 8, "Blessed are the pure in heart," etc. At this meeting the people of Falling Spring petitioned that Mr. Caven may be forwarded in his trials for ordination, and that they might have his answer to their call, and he was allowed until next meeting to make answer.

In April 1739 Presbytery met, when Mr. Caven delivered a Lecture on Psalm 133:1, "Behold how good and how pleasant it is for brethren to dwell together in unity" which was approved. He also read a discourse upon the perspicuity of the Scripture which was approved. Presbytery then requiring his answer to the call from Falling Spring he accepted it.

At a meeting in June he opened the sessions with an exercise on Romans viii. 8, "So then they that are in the flesh cannot please God" "according to appointment, which is approved as part of trial." He was appointed to deliver at next meeting a Popular Sermon on Heb. xii. 14, "Follow peace with all men" etc., which he did September 4, 1739 at the meeting at Chestnut Level.

At the meeting October 10, 1739 a Committee consisting of Messrs. Anderson, Boyd, and Craighead was appointed to ordain and install Messrs. Caven and Thompson. The Committee met at Silver Spring, i. e., Lower Pennsboro, November 14th, and ordained and installed Mr. Thompson. On the 16th they met here. The Committee consisted of Messrs. Anderson, Boyd, Craighead and Sam'l. Thompson just ordained. On their meeting at the church, "the Rev. Mr. Boyd having published an edict at the door in the hearing of both parties, Thos. Brown appeared and declared that if said societies are willing to have Mr. Caven ordained among them he would make no objection against it. Mr. Anderson then preached from 1 Tim. vl. 6 "But thou, O man of God, flee these things," etc, and presided in the ordination of Mr. Caven. He was also installed as pastor of this church, thus becoming the first pastor of the East Conococheague charges i. e., of Falling Spring and Greencastle, November 16th, 1739.

There is no record of the parts taken by the other members of the Committee in these services. "It was agreed at this meeting that the other house of worship should be at Falling Spring."

We have said that Mr. Caven was the first pastor of our church. The author of the book called "The Churches of the Valley," in view of the following which appears in the Minutes of Presbytery, concludes that Mr. Samuel Thompson must have preceded him here. This is the record: "Richard O. Cohen, Jos. Armstrong, Benj. Chambers, and Patrick Jack, have publicly engaged to pay Mr. Sam'l. Thompson the sum of £1 s5 at or before next meeting of Presbytery as being the whole of arrears due him by the people at Conococheague." It has been inferred from this that Mr. Thompson was pastor before Mr. Caven. But the Minutes make no mention of this. As stated already Mr. Thompson and Mr. Caven were both appointed to supply alternately at Pennsboro and Conococheague, and these arrears were due to him, no doubt, as supply.

When Mr. Caven's settlement had been agreed upon, the Commissioner, Jas. Lindsay, was asked by Presbytery what provision they had made for his sustenance among them. He said that the subscription "amounted to £46 which they will increase, and what can be had over and above shall be allowed him, and that they will do what they can to procure him a plantation to live upon." He stated also that the people had agreed about the bounds between them and the West side of Conococheague.

Mr. Caven remained pastor until July 2, 1741 when he resigned.

He was called then to Goodwill, Orange County, N. Y., and, after laboring there for some time, he came back to this region. I cannot learn whether he was settled as pastor of Goodwill or was simply what we now call a stated supply. On returning to this section he seems to have itinerated for a time, to have then gone to Virginia, and finally to have preached at Silver Spring in Cumberland county, where he died and was buried November 2, 1750, at the age of 44.

Our church seems to have made no attempts for a long time to secure a pastor after Mr. Caven left it. It had had, however, a fair measure of supplies. A great misfortune befell the Presbytery many years ago in the loss of a volume of its Minutes, covering the period from October 1750–1759. It was loaned by the Stated Clerk to a minister in the South before the war, and has never been returned. Of course we can learn nothing of our church during those nine years.

Referring to the Minutes again we find that it was supplied from 1741–1750 by Presbytery, and by some ministers who came to itinerate within its bounds Messrs. Craighead, Thompson, McDowell, Sankey, Black and Caven, are mentioned as having supplied our congregation. It will be remembered that Mr. Caven gave up the charge in 1741, and lived until 1750. The next reference to our church appears in the Minutes of a meeting held at Upper Marsh Creek, August 12, 1760. "Supplication for supply was brought in from East Conococheague, Falling Spring, West Conococheague, etc. Accordingly Mr. Williamson is appointed to preach at Falling Spring. In October Mr. Thompson is appointed to preach."

In 1761, April 28, supplications came from Falling Spring for supplies, and Messrs. Duffield and Beard are sent. So in 1762, in April and November, supplications both written and verbal came from our church. In 1763 a Mr. McGaw was sent to preach. In 1764 a Mr. Slemmons was appointed our supply. In 1766 came a request to Presbytery for supplies from Rocky Spring and Falling Spring and for a minister to ordain elders sometime before the administration of the Lord's Supper. In October 14th, is another request for supplies, and I find no other reference to our church until the year 1771. By this I mean that the name of Falling Spring does not appear in the list of churches seeking supplies. The name of East Conococheague frequently appears, and it may be that we come in with Greencastle under that name.

The church was thus supplied in their irregular way until the year 1769 when the Rev. Jas. Long or Lang took charge of these two congregations. The following minute appears in the record ot the meeting of Presbytery June 20, 1764. "Mr. Jas. Long a licensed candidate from the 2d Presbytery of Philadelphia asked to be taken under the care of this Presbytery. His credentials from the 2d Presbytery read and approved, and upon his promised subjection to us in the Lord, the Presbytery cheerfully receive him under our care, and appoint him to open our next Presbytery." This he did October 23d with a sermon from 2 Cor. v. 21, "He hath made Him to be sin for us" etc. The next year he was invited by the churches of York and Shrewsbury to supply them for one year, which he agreed to do, and he was appointed by Presbytery as their supply until the close of the Presbyterial year in April 1767.

In 1765 the Donegal Presbytery had been divided, and that of Carlisle constituted for a part of it. This arrangement lasted but a year. By the act of Synod in 1786 the old Donegal was again divided into the Presbyteries of Baltimore and Carlisle. The church was much disturbed by these new arrangements, and feeling ran very high. Mr. Lang seems to have been dissatisfied, and to have either labored little in this region, or to have gone, for a time, elsewhere. The only reference to him from 1767–69 is to a sermon preached by him here, July 1768, on Gal. II. 21. "If righteousness come by the Law then Christ is dead in vain." In the Minute of 1769 we have this, "Rev. Jas. Lang being present declared his desire to be received as a member of this Presbytery, according to the terms granted by Synod at the last meeting, and having renounced his declinature, as specified in the Synod's Minutes, respecting that affair as far as he was concerned in it, he is admitted as a member. I find no record of his call to our church, or of his installation as pastor. But the statement is made by one or two authors in writing up this ancient history, that he was installed pastor of East Conococheague and Falling Spring, thus dividing his time between Greencastle and us, he living in Greencastle. In 1770 the record is, that Mr. Lang had not fulfilled his appointments at the last Spring meeting, and regretting that the people had been disappointed, he declares his resolution to be more punctual for the future. In April 1771 he was chosen Moderator for the year. The record of a meeting held in August in Tuscarora, Virginia, is "Mr. Lang is now come, and takes his seat as Moderator. His Elder is Mr. William Cross." I quote this because it is the first reference to the presence in Presbytery of an Elder of his. Whether he came from Greencastle or from this church is not stated. It may be noted, as an item of interest here, that Presbytery met in our church June, 1776, just one month previous to the Declaration of Independence.

Mr. Lang continued to serve the East Conococheague charge until 1793. In the Minutes of Presbytery, session at Lower Marsh Creek, October, 1792, in this record, "A supplication was presented by the united congregations of Falling Spring and East Conococheague requesting that Mr. Speer be appointed for six months statedly to supply them, in rotation with their pastor. Mr. Lang declares his hearty consent to this." Accordingly when supplies were appointed we read, "Mr. Speer to supply Mr. Lang's Congregation three months between this and next spring meeting." It is of interest to observe, in passing, that at this meeting the name of David Denny first appears, he having been appointed to give supplies in different parts of the Presbytery. While Mr. Speer was considering this invitation to labor for six months in connection with Mr. Lang, a meeting of Presbytery was held and the following is part of its record.

"Carlisle, April, 1794, an instrument in writing from the congregation of Falling Spring was laid before Presbytery, which is as follows: 'At a meeting of the congregation held at the Court House in Chambersburg on April, 7, 1794, pursuant to notice from the pulpit, it was agreed that the congregation, taking into consideration the proposed call to Mr. Speer, and viewing their present situation as more favorable than when said call was signed, and also having good assurance of their increasing ability, have unanimously resolved to advance the sum promised in said call to the sum of of 175 pounds. Resolved, that Benjamin Chambers and Andrew Dunlop be appointed to attend on Presbytery as Commissioners in the prosecution of said call.

JOHN SCOTT, President.

Attest: WM. BROWN, Secretary.' "

. Mr. Speer accepted the call at this meeting, He had already been called to Edisto Island, South Carolina, and to Plattsburg, N. Y., in 1793.

In October Presbytery met in our church in this place, heard his trial sermons in which "he acquitted himself to their satisfaction." He was then ordained and installed pastor. The sermon on this occasion was by a Mr. Snodgrass from 2 Thess. III:1, "Brethren, pray for us, that the word of the Lord may have free course, and be glorified." Rev. Mr. McPherrin of Hagerstown presided, and gave the charge to pastor and people. Mr. Speer was a graduate of Dickenson College, studying there under Dr. Nesbit, was taken under care of Presbytery April, 1790, was licensed June 22, 1791, and in October was ordained and settled here. He continued to serve the church until 1797, when, at his request the relation was dissolved.* Presbytery supplied

---

* EXTRACT FROM THE MINUTES OF PRESBYTERY APRIL 12, 1797.—"Mr. Speer applied for leave to resign his pastoral charge of Falling Spring, and Presbytery after hearing his reasons, and the representation of Messrs. John Scott, John

the church until 1800 when it secured the services of Mr. David Denny. The minute in his case reads thus: "October, 1790, Session at Falling Spring.

"Messrs. McLane, Boyd and Denny appeared and proposed themselves to be taken under care of Presbytery on trials for the Gospel ministry. Presbytery found that they had obtained a regular college education; had spent some time in study of divinity; were of unblemished moral character; and, having conversed with them to a considerable length with regard to their views, and their experience of religion on their own souls; agreed to take them on trial."

Mr. Denny was licensed October 6th, 1791, at the meeting at Rocky Spring. In April, 1793, he was called to Path Valley, and was ordained and installed there April, 1794. At that meeting Mr. Speer accepted the call to our church. In October, 1800, Mr. Denny was called to be pastor of Falling Spring and was installed on the last Monday of November. In the service Dr. King presided, Dr. Cooper preached, and Mr. Francis Herron (later Dr. Herron of the First Church, Pittsburg) gave the charges. Mr. Denny continued pastor until 1838, thus making the long pastorate of 37 years. Dr. Wing in his sermon says of him, "he was manly and conservative, candid and sincere, always found at the post of duty, and beloved to the last by his grateful people." The Session during his pastorate consisted of John King, David Lytle, Moses Kirkpatrick, W. S. Davis, Robert McCracken, Samuel Blood, Samuel Cooper, Samuel McElroy, Robert Sharpe. I have not found any list of trustees.

In 1878, Tuesday, May 28, a two-storied brick building

Halliday, John Crawford, and Wm. Brotherton, Commissioners from said congregation, agreed to dismiss him, and Mr. Speer is hereby dismissed."
  LIST OF COMMUNICANTS IN JOHN CRAWFORD'S DISTRICT IN REV. MR. SPEER'S CONGREGATION, OCTOBER 16, 1795.—John Crawford, Ann Crawford, Edward Crawford, Elizabeth Crawford. Alex. McKean, Elizabeth McKean, Effie Hill, John Beard, Martha Beard, David Morehead, Martha Morehead, James McWilliams, Mary McWilliams, John McWilliams.

which had long been used for Sabbath School purposes, and for a Lecture room, gave place to the stone chapel which was built in the same year and at a cost of $9,000.

There was for many years a mission school made up of the colored people of the town which met in the basement of the old Lecture room. It was under the care largely of Mr. W. G. Reed, and prospered to a remarkable degree. The teachers were chiefly from our own church, though a number came from the other congregations of the town. Some time after the old building had been torn down, the church rented the basement of the Bethel church which stands at the western end of Queen street on the Western Maryland railroad, and the school met there. In December 21, 1890, we put up the neat frame building in which it is taught now on West Loudon street.

It is with great pleasure that we have with us to-day the Central Presbyterian church of the town, and it will be in place here to refer to its origin.

Finding in 1868 that we needed more church room the question arose whether we should enlarge this building or colonize. Many were opposed to making any great change in our venerable house of worship, while some favored it. These brethren who did so sent a petition to Presbytery for a second organization which was granted. On the 15th of August the Session gave 28 certficates of dismissal, and on the same day (Saturday) the Committee appointed by Presbytery arrived and the church was organized. The committee was composed of the Rev. Dr. Thos. Creigh, Rev. W. A. West, and Elder Craig McLanahan.

Messrs. J. C. Austin and James Reside were chosen Elders, and were ordained on the Sabbath, Dr. Creigh preaching in the morning and Mr. West in the evening. Their church has been greatly blessed of God, and I speak for us here of the mother church when I say that we wish it well with all our heart, and that we ask of the Saviour for it the best He has to give.

Thus has the Lord led on our church and we look back now over the chequered way with gratitude. For a century and a half at least has the light been shining on this hill. So long has the standard for the truth been lifted up here. This ancient church has kept the faith once delivered to the saints. It has so happened—so far as I can find—that the men who have preached to it and watched it for God, have believed the doctrines taught in the Confession of Faith. I do not think that this church and Session would tolerate any man in this pulpit who would preach another Gospel than that which has always been preached here. "Thus saith the Lord, stand ye in the ways and see; and ask for the old paths where is the good way, and walk therein and ye shall find rest for your soul." Jer. VI: 16.

"Now unto Him who is able to keep you from falling and to present you faultless before the presence of His glory with exceeding joy; to the only wise God our Saviour be glory and majesty, dominion and power, both now and ever." Amen.

THE REV. J. G. HIBBEN'S PAPER.

To the Congregation of the Falling Spring Church:—

This is the season which by common consent we consecrate to memory. The pictures of the present with their wealth of meaning, the richness of their coloring, the intermingling of light and shade, their subtle suggestions to our hope, and to our love, all this is owing to the fact that we are laying the past under mighty tribute to the present.

The actual is thus ever idealized by the after-glow which streams upon it from the fires of the past. Living as you do at the close of this century of light, standing in the foremost files of time, possessing the heritage of a noble history, both civil and ecclesiastical, this becomes not only a time of congratulation and thanksgiving but an occasion also replete with inspiration. It is the privilege of each one of you to exclaim with that rare German poet:

"My inheritance, how wide and fair,
Time is my vast seedfield; of Time I'm heir."

That I have had a part, however small, in your history, I have always regarded as a privilege and honor. And our relation as pastor and people has a special significance for me, inasmuch as this has been my first, and always will be my only pastoral charge. It is to me personally a matter of special interest that I was ordained in this church, and inducted into the pastoral office by the Presbytery, of which a hundred years ago my great-great-grandfather, Dr. Cooper of the Middle Spring Church, was a life-long member. Thus I am united to you by ancestral as well as ecclesiastical ties.

But there are ties far stronger than friendship. And to you with whom I worked in a common cause for four years, I am bound with cords that neither time nor space can sever. Among all the memories of this Church, the most grateful is the consciousness that I have friends firm and true, whose love and sympathetic interest I cherish ever as a priceless possession. When I think of you, and our past together, my heart is warmed. As the odor of a flower will often make vivid and real some far away past, so now, the fragrant flower of friendship brings to me with its rare perfume a rush of thought that re-establishes for a while the days that are gone, and recalls with an old time distinctness the scenes endeared by a thousand strong associations.

> "So muse I of old times, old homes, old friends.
> Old friends, the uniting of those words has borne
> My fancy backward to the gracious past,
> The generous past, when all was possible,
> For all was then untried; the years between
> Have taught some sweet, some bitter lessons; none
> Wiser than this—to spend in all things else,
> But of old friends to be most miserly."

Always, and at a time of reunion especially, do we miss the many whose friendship has become to us a holy thing, because they are with God. We claim them still as ours; for we are God's, as they are His. We feel their presence near. The very insistence of our desire makes them real to our hearts. The memory of their sweet strong lives stirs within us hallowed feelings of a solemn joy. Many of you through this celebration may have had some such experience as that of the aged man who found himself one time upon the banks of the Rhine, at a spot which had been peculiarly associated with two companions of his earlier days, and who as he crosses the river, sits deep bowed in reverie, until reaching the opposite shore, when he exclaims:—

> "Take, O boatman, thrice thy fee,
> Take, I give it willingly;
> For, invisible to thee
> Spirits twain have crossed with me."

It is easy to shut the eyes and with memory's inner vision, see old forms, and old faces along these aisles and in these pews; and to recognize perchance, the touch of a vanished hand, or the sound of a voice that is still.

We are thus ever and again reminded that the brotherhood of which we are all members, persists through all separation, be it even that of death.

It is to me ever a grateful thought, that though called to work in other fields, I am still one with you in your labors here, for ours is one work—the search after the truth, and the endeavor to promote the cause of righteousness alway and everywhere. And we feel constrained at such a time as this, to dedicate ourselves anew to its high behests and sacred trusts. While celebrating this festival which commemorates the history of this Church for a hundred years and more, it seems to me well to recall to mind, that we are members of a still greater brotherhood,—the holy catholic church of Christ. All denominational and local pride is merged in that larger loyalty, and freer, broader spirit of fraternity which spring up in our hearts with the thought, that ours is the Church whose history stretches back through the centuries to the Manger of Bethlehem, when the Shepherds fed their flocks by night hard by upon the hills of David; and whose future will reveal a still more glorious destiny, in its progressive march towards that

> "One far off, divine event
> To which the whole creation moves."

It is meet, therefore, that, realizing the splendor of our heritage, we join heart and voice in ascribing unto Christ Jesus, the Head of the church universal, all honor and glory. "For thou, O Christ, art the King of Glory; Thou art the everlasting Son of the Father. Heaven and earth are full of the majesty of Thy glory; The glorious company of the Apostles praise Thee; The goodly fellowship of the prophets praise Thee; The noble army of martyrs praise Thee; The Holy Church throughout all the world doth acknowledge Thee."

REMARKS OF THE REV. J. A. CRAWFORD, D. D.

I have been asked to refer to any facts or incidents in connection with my ministry here which may, perhaps, be of interest on an occasion like this. It is not easy to do this at this late date, and inasmuch as I have no connected account to which to refer.

I may say something in regard to the experiences of our church in the great Revival of Religion which God graciously granted here in the years seventy-six and seventy-seven. In the autumn and early winter of seventy-six, times of refreshing from the presence of the Lord came to many sections of our land. Churches here and there began to show a deepened interest in the welfare of this lost world, and great concern lest men should perish. I cannot remember what it was that led to this. But the fact is as stated. Some of us can recall the great revival of fifty-seven, and what it was that told upon the churches then. News came from India of the terrible mutiny there among the Sepoy troops of the British army. We read with horror of the massacre at Cawnpore and Lucknow, of the butchery of our missionaries by the Nana Sahib. All Britain was greatly moved and shocked, and our own land as well. The church waked to realize that she had been sadly neglectful of her duty to the heathen, and that, so far from pushing the great work of Foreign Missions, she had, in fact, been toying with it, and that now God was rebuking and admonishing her in a very positive way indeed. She turned, therefore, to the Lord with confession, and with renewal of her covenant, and set herself with new zeal to her high task. The result was her general revival. And we in this country shared in it. I well remember the state of things in my own church in southern Ohio, and the many who turned to the Lord. But I cannot now account for the general interest which in 1876 began to show itself all over our land in the cause of lost men. There was plainly some blessed power at work and our churches here were conscious of it. You will remember that meetings were held by our two congregations in the Central church and in our own by turns. The Rev. Dr. Caldwell was pastor then of the Central. For weeks the meetings were continued, and the result was that fifty-seven united with our own church on profession of their faith. Of these ten were heads of families. The session appointed a meeting (1) for the young men by themselves, (2) for the young women, (3) for the heads of families. So that when the Sabbath of Communion came there was the large number which I have just given applying for admission. It was a time of great joy to us all. Some came back to the Lord who had wandered away. Family altars were set up in many a home, and the meetings for prayer were often crowded. It was delightful to watch the increasing change in the manner of life of some of those who at that time came into the church. Not only were they in their seats in the meeting for prayer, but many of them, in a timid yet a manly Christian way, began to take a part in the services. When opportunity was given to speak or to offer prayer it was seized by one and another. I remember with what interest I listened as they spoke to us, or to God for us. It must have been a great trial to some of them who were not used to public speaking. And we were edified.

In the cases of some of these brethren there were points of great interest. I well remember the experience of one of them. He was a man of great intellectual force, very logical and acute. His heart must needs be reached through his head. He would have been glad to get to the Lord in a merely logical way had that been possible, and to find Him simply by the Reason. I felt myself embarrassed in talking with him. I did not doubt his sincerity. I could see his spiritual uneasiness, that he was weary of himself and of his methods as one who was seeking to be saved. I remember how we walked the pavement in the night, he pressing me to make things plain if I could. This state of things continued until I began to think that he never would be the Lord's, and come to Him on His own terms. But finally he did. It must have been that the Spirit taught him and powerfully persuaded him,—for I was at my limit. And I am sure that to-day he would not for all the world be back at his old halting place of doubt, nor take any other way to the sky, even supposing one could be opened, than the one he did take of simple, believing submission to God.

I recall the case of another, and he too a man of mind. He was of a reverent spirit, sincere, conscientious. But he could not make up his mind. I had several interviews and prayers with him, and he was ready to confess the Lord. But he allowed the opportunity to pass, hoping to see more clearly than he did in his twilight, and finally he came.

I remember—perhaps it was about this time—that I preached a sermon, and which because of the interest which the curious theme had for me, I have sometimes thought that I would repeat, on the words in 2 Kings VII: 7, 'Wherefore they arose and fled in the twilight.' The theme was that if we fly for safety at all we must run with the twilight views we have. Some of you may recall the text if not the sermon.

In the revival time of the winter of seventy-six and the spring of seventy-seven we had in the old Lecture-room some most enjoyable and precious seasons. I remember the meetings for the young men, our kneeling and prayer together. Then they had meetings conducted by themselves and on which neither pastor nor elder intruded.

The Rev. Geo. B. Needham, an evangelist, came on invitation of the churches and spent some time in preaching the Gospel, his wife leading Bible readings with the ladies. They were good people, we thought, and we put no hindrance in their way, but gave them every opportunity to do good.

We had a fine opportunity in the session at that time when so many as fifty-seven were inquiring for the way, to learn what it was that led those who came to seek the Lord. And we could see and did see by how a seemingly small circumstance a man's eternal fate may be determined. Some traced their first good impression to a sermon, or to a casual occurance, or to some word of Scripture. Some could give no connected account of the beginning of their new experience. It mattered not. The Holy Spirit was plainly at work along his ordinary lines and the blessed results were reached.

REMARKS OF THE REV. S. J. NICCOLLS, D. D.

(The following is a summary taken from the local papers as reported at the time, Dr. Niccolls having written that he was unable to furnish a copy:)

Dr. Niccolls said, he was invited to supply the church in 1860. After preaching on two Sabbaths he was extended a call. He found he was in his right place, and thought there never was a charge so dear. It was his first charge. The church was one of peculiar standing. Here were the leading men of this community, men prominent in the state, foremost at the bar and in the practice of medicine. The circumstances which led to the first revival after his coming were singular. He desired one evening to speak to a member of the choir on spiritual matters, but was prevented by a rehearsal. While talking to a young lawyer, who afterward entered the ministry, (the Rev. Dr. Orr,) a message came to him that a man had been injured on the Cumberland Valley Railroad. He went to the old station to see the man. On entering, he saw on the wall the Superintendent's order, "Passengers must purchase tickets before starting." He wondered if the man, who in the morning, boastful of his great physical strength, had reviled religion, had procured his ticket; he found he had not. He preached a very plain funeral sermon over the man's remains. The discourse had much effect, and a revival began. Services were held night after night, and as a result some fifty were gathered into the church. Among other things growing out of this revival was the increased activity of the young people. * * * * * The best definition of faith he ever heard was from the lips of an old colored woman here: "God said he would save me and I'm a-holdin' Him to it!" Dr. Niccolls said: "Could I put events in their true historical sequence the result would be entrancing in its harmony—the music of God's people moving forward." Dr. Niccolls illustrated the value of prayer by this incident: After the fire when it was reported that rebels were returning, and people were fleeing from the town, he was left alone with his wife and his only daughter, who was so ill that a ride on the train would almost certainly cause her death. He took the little child in his arms, went into his study, and prayed the Lord to give her strength to be removed from town on a train which was to leave several hours afterward. Then he replaced the child in her carriage. For a few moments she slept, and then awoke and tried to get out of her carriage. She was not interfered with, and presently climbed from it, and walking to her toys began to play with them. He knew then that his prayer had been answered, and they left Chambersburg that afternoon. * * * * Dr. Niccolls concluded as follows: "The true genius of the child of God is to walk in the hope of better times. Your best days are before you. No true child of God turns to the past and moans and groans over what has gone from him. More thrilling days are before us. The twentieth century has more glory to unfold to us than the marvelous nineteenth."

PERSONAL HISTORY OF THE PASTORS.

I.

REV. SAMUEL CAVEN, 1739 TO 1741.

Samuel Caven, the first Pastor of the Falling Spring Church, was born in 1706, and came to this country from Templerea, county Tyrone, Ireland, not long prior to 1737. The earliest reference to him in the Minutes of the Presbytery of Donegal, which then included the territory of our Church, bears the date of October 5, 1737. On that day Mr. Caven, in company with Mr. John Elder, a licentiate of New Castle Presbytery, "having produced sufficient testimonials and having preached to the satisfaction of Presbytery, and adopted the Westminster Confession of Faith, and Catechism, as the confession of their faith, and promised obedience to Presbytery, were taken under its care." Mr. Caven was at once appointed to supply the people of Pennsborough (now Silver Spring) the first three Sabbaths of October. On November 6, 1737, Presbytery sent him to Conococheague or Clear Water Settlement, "embracing what is now Falling Spring, Upper West Conococheague, (Mercersburg), East Conococheague, or Greencastle, and Lower West Conococheague, or Welsh Run." He acted as supply for these four Churches and the Churches of Pennsborough (alternating every four Sabbaths with Mr. Samuel Thomson), until April 12, 1738, when Presbytery was requested to arrange for Mr. Thomson to be called to both the societies of Pennsborough. For the balance of two years, Mr. Caven supplied the Conococheague churches alone, when those four churches were separated by Presbytery into two charges. At the same time he was appointed by Presbytery to supply at Upper Hopewell and Middle Spring, at the meeting of Presbytery April 20, 1739. Mr. Caven having received and accepted a call from the East Side, comprising the present Falling Spring and Greencastle churches, he was ordained and installed November 16, 1739. On November 17, Presbytery ordered that he should supply Upper Hopewell or Middle Spring on certain Sabbaths in December, 1739, and February and March, 1740. On June 18, 1740, he was appointed to supply Great Conewago, and Lower Marsh Creek on the first Sabbath of July and "to preach there on a week day and inquire into the state of both these settlements and make a report at our next." And in September, he was appointed to supply again on fixed days. During the winter of 1740-41, he visited the Churches and settlements on the South Branch of the Potomac. On the 2nd of July, 1741, at his own request, he was dismissed from the Falling Spring charge. During the summer he spent some time at Antietam (or Hagerstown), Marsh Creek, Opequhon, and on the South Branch.

It was while he was still Pastor at Falling Spring, that the famous Craighead Case came before the Synod of Philadelphia, in May, 1741. It would be a long story to tell. Suffice it to say, as we are confined to the *personal* history of the Pastors of this Church, that Mr. Caven was one of the twelve signers of the Protestation presented to Synod on June 1st. And the Protestation was the final occasion of the rupture of 1741, when the Synod was divided into Old Side and New Side, a rupture which Dr. Charles Hodge (Constitutional History, Vol. 2, pages 158-9,) characterizes as "a disorderly rupture, when not even the forms of an ecclesiastical, much less of a judicial proceeding, were observed." That rupture appears to have been caused, not so much by doctrinal differences as by the state and needs of the church. On the Old Side, it was charged, were an orthodox faith frozen into a dead formalism, and a consequent or accompanying lack of spiritually-minded preachers of sufficient education to maintain the old and well-established grade of intelligence in the Presbyterian ministry, while at the same time earnest and consecrated enough to meet the increasing demand for revived and practical piety. The New Side were for such men and measures as would result in a revival of godliness while maintaining a high grade of education. On the Old Side were to be found men like Robert Cross, John Thomson, Francis Alison, John Elder, and Samuel Caven. On the New Side were arrayed the William Tennents, senior and junior, Gilbert Tennent, Alexander Craighead and David Alexander (the two latter of the Presbytery of Donegal), Charles Tennent and Samuel Blair, who had also the moral support of the great Whitefield.

The above facts shed not a little light on the position of the Falling Spring Pastor, Samuel Caven, and of the Church itself, upon the questions agitating the Church at large. Samuel Caven, taking his stand with the Old Side, finds himself at variance with a part of his Falling Spring charge, which was New Side to so considerable an extent that Gillett says "his people complained of him that he never asked about the state of their souls," and another writer, that "he was much complained of by them, as not sufficiently anxious for their salvation, and as failing in pointed conversation and preaching in regard to their spiritual state." On this account he was released from this charge. And from this it may be inferred that the Falling Spring Church in its very earliest history was to a large degree ranged on the New Side, and advocated such methods of worship as those by which the great Tennents and the greater Whitefield sought to revive the church and bring sinners to Christ.

Mr. Caven on leaving this field, as I have already said, while without a regular charge from 1741–9 itinerated in various places under appointment by Presbytery. It appears that in May, 1743, he was called to the Church at Goodwill, N. Y. He also visited vacant Churches in Virginia and other States. He occasionally supplied the Falling Spring Church and the Greencastle (then Lower East Conococheague), and was invited to the latter Church November 6, 1744, but declined the call. On April 4, 1749, he was called to the Lower Pennsborough (now Silver Spring) Church, and "their vacancy for four years had produced such a desire for the settlement of a Pastor that they sent with the call a supplication, earnestly requesting Mr. Caven's speedy acceptance." Having accepted the call, he was installed at Silver Spring, August 5, 1749, the Rev. Richard Sanckey presiding and preaching from the text, Prov. 11:30, "The fruit of the righteous is a tree of life, and he that winneth souls is wise." Mr. Caven's pastorate was brief. He died November 9, 1750, aged 44 years. A tombstone marks his resting-place in the Silver Spring burying-ground.

Tradition says that Mr. Caven never married.

From the date of Mr. Caven's release from the Falling Spring charge, July 2, 1741, until the installation of Rev. James Lang, in 1767, we know little or nothing of the ministers who preached in this Church. Mr. Caven was appointed at times, as June 10, 1744, to supply the pulpit. The Records of Presbytery, for the years 1750–59 have been lost. It would seem that no settled Pastor labored here during that period. At any rate, we must pass on and notice briefly the life and work of

II.

REV. JAMES LANG, 1767 TO 1793.

Mr. Lang was born in Ireland, in 1737, and came to this country in early manhood. In 1764 he was married to Margaret Helm, of Lancaster, Pa.

Mr. Lang's pastorate here covered the entire period of the American Revolution. Some facts of interest in regard to his pastorate have been preserved to us. The Old and New Sides having reunited in 1758, peace for a time reigned. So much so that Mr. Lang, an Old Side sympathizer, could be Pastor for twenty-six years of a Church which had had strong New Side leanings, as this had when Mr. Caven, also of the Old Side, was released from the charge twenty-six years earlier. Yet the old spirit of difference was still present. The Presbytery of Carlisle, composed mostly of New Side men, was erected by the Synod in 1765 and had a brief existence. The dissatisfaction was not quieted or removed. In 1766 the Old Presbytery of Donegal was revived. Peace did not yet come. In 1767, the records show, some dissatisfied brethren proceeded to form themselves into a separate body, and to act in a Presbyterial capacity. One of their earliest acts directly touched this Church. For this independent Presbytery ordained James Lang and installed him Pastor of the East Conococheague (or Greencastle) and Falling Spring Churches! Thus it came about that the second Pastor of this Church was ordained and put in charge by a self-constituted body of men acting in rebellion to the Synod, men who were representatives of the Old Side element, and now exercising authority in a church which had formerly compelled an Old Side minister to resign his charge! Such are the changes which come over Churches in the course of years. And Synod, at the same meeting in 1767, adopted a resolution that this self-constituted Presbytery "must not now be considered members of this body." And in the list of ministers named, Mr. Lang's name is not found. In June, 1767, the Synod's Presbytery of Donegal adopted similar resolutions against the indepentent Presbytery of Donegal. In 1768, however, Synod, "for the sake of peace" authorized its Presbytery of Donegal to receive Messrs. Thomson and Lang, "provided they apply for admission the first convenient opportunity." A similar provision was adopted as to the other ministers concerned. April 11, 1769, Mr. Lang, at his own request, was so received and enrolled by the Donegal Presbytery. Thus it came about that both Synod and Presbytery recognized the ordination of Mr. Lang, although done by a self-constituted and rebellious body.

Mr. Lang remained Pastor of this Church from 1767 until November 4, 1793, residing in Greencastle, and preaching here once in two weeks. On the latter date he was released from this charge. The reason for his leaving the pastorate of this Church was that charges against him had been presented in Presbytery, by members of this Church, alleging that he was accustomed to use light and trifling language in his sermons. He was acquited of these charges, but offered his resignation. He still retained his position as Pastor of the Old Side portion of the Lower East Conococheague or Greencastle Church, which itself had some time before divided into Old and New Side. In the Old Side portion of the latter charge he remained Pastor until November 26, 1800. During his pastorate at Falling Spring, he was with others appointed in April, 1775, to supply some of the vacant and new churches in the Presbytery. During his pastorate this congregation was incorporated, March 25, 1785, by the name of "The Trustees of the Presbyterian Church of Falling Spring, in the County of Franklin."

One item of interest has been brought to light, in seeking for information about our Church during this period. Prof. J. W. Mears, D. D., is our authority for the statement, as he gave it in an address on "The Presbyterian Element in Our National Life and History," before the old Synod of Central New York, at Watertown, October 18, 1876. In that address Prof. Mears shows how Presbyterianism allied itself, identified itself with the cause of free government, and goes on to say: "of the Scotch-Irish race in America it is said it is perhaps the only race of all that settled in the western world that never produced one Tory. The nearest case to it ever known was that of a man who was brought before a church session in Chambersburg, and tried upon the charge that he was not sincere in his profession of his attachment to the cause of the Revolution." It has not been so far possible to discover the name of this man. Perhaps it is just as well to let it rest in obscurity. Prof. Mears makes another statement which will interest us, when he says: "It is claimed that General Washington, when making a long and disheartening retreat, was asked where he expected to pause. He replied, that if he was obliged to cross every river and every mountain to the limits of civilization, he would make his last stand with the Scotch-Irishmen of the frontiers, there plant his banner and still fight for freedom."

We are indebted to the Rev. J. P. Barbor, of Burlington, Kansas, a great-grandson of Mr. Lang, for the following most interesting information:

"I have a dozen of my great-grandfather's manuscript sermons preached at Falling Spring Church, also the silk stockings he wore when he was married to Margaret Helm in Lancaster City in 1764, when they wore knee-breeches. I have, also, a description of him by a man who taught in his family and who very greatly esteemed him. He represents him as having been in appearance like Andrew Jackson and a fine preacher. His oldest daughter, Mary, was married to John Park, a stepson of Colonel Johnson. John Park secured a large tract of good land in Indiana county, where with Colonel Johnson he had been surveying for the state, and there he lived and died somewhat prematurely in 1844. His wife, my mother's mother, was a grand old woman and lived to raise a large family of her own and several adopted orphans. I think it is stated that for fifty years she did not miss a Communion at the old Gilgal Church where she belonged, though it is four miles away.

"One of the sermons of which I have written was preached on the first Thanksgiving day after the Revolutionary war and another was preached on the day of humiliation and prayer observed after the death of General Washington." The former has been published and a copy of it filed among the archives of the Falling Spring Church. Mr. Lang frequently supplied this pulpit for several years after the relation as pastor was dissolved, April, 1797.

The Rev. Mr. Barbor has two manuscript sermons preached by Mr. Lang in this Church, one on John 20: 29, "The Nature of Saving Faith," preached the second Sabbath of September, 1768; the other on Luke 9: 55, "The Necessity of Knowing Ourselves," preached the second Sabbath of April, 1781. Mr. Lang died at his home about three miles northwest of Greencastle in 1818. Ten years previous to his death he lost his eyesight entirely.

III.

WILLIAM SPEER, 1794 TO 1797.

We have now reached a point where more definite and detailed information is at hand. For much of this I am indebted to the Rev. William Speer, D. D., of Washington,

Pa., grandson of the first Pastor of this Church as a separate charge, and the third in the history of the Church.

William Speer, was born September 15, 1764, at the Gap of the South Mountain, eight miles west of Gettysburg. His father, James Speer, came from the north of Ireland in 1759, with his family, accompanied by two brothers. Elizabeth, a daughter of James, was married to James Buchanan, merchant, of Mercersburg. James, one of her sons, became President of the United States.

William, the subject of this sketch, was the youngest son of James Speer. He began the study of Latin at the school of the Rev. Alexander Dobbin, in Gettysburg. (Mr. Dobbin lived in a house at the foot of Cemetery Hill, within the battle-field of July 1-3, 1863.) Young Speer was received into the membership of the Lower Marsh Creek Church, probably under the pastorate of the Rev. John McKnight, which began in 1783. He was graduated from Dickinson College, May 7, 1788, and studied theology there in a class taught by the celebrated Rev. Dr. Charles Nesbit, whom Dr. Witherspoon, when first invited from Scotland to the presidency of Princeton College, recommended instead of himself, for that position, as the most suitable person within his knowledge. Mr. Speer was a favorite student of Dr. Nesbit.

June 9, 1791, he was licensed to preach by the Presbytery of Carlisle, with permission to labor in New York, where he was for a few months associated with the Rev. Dr. John Rodgers and the Rev. Dr. John McKnight in the Collegiate (First) Dutch Reformed Church, which embraced the Wall Street, Brick, and Rutgers Street Churches. On leaving this work, he made extensive evangelistic tours during 1792–3, as far as northern New York and Charleston, S. C., preaching also in New Jersey and Pennsylvania. He refused calls to Edisto Island, S. C., and Plattsburg, N. Y. In 1793, before his ordination as a minister, the General Assembly appointed him as "Missionary for two months from New York to the East Branch of the Susquehanna, at a salary of $33.33 a month."

About the close of the year 1793, he was called to the Falling Spring Church, at a salary of 160 pounds sterling per annum, afterwards, before his acceptance of the call, increased to 175 pounds. He began to preach regularly for this people January 24, 1794. "The communities of Carlisle and Chambersburg and of that portion of the state were composed of people of much intelligence and refinement. As Scotch-Irishmen, they held to the old truths of their Church, yet some few were infected with the French infidelity and general irreligious spirit which prevailed among that class in the time before the Revolutionary War and the 'Great Revival of 1800.' The language of the Pastoral Letter of our General Assembly in 1798 describes the condition of society and of the Churches then as fearfully derelict in religious principles and filled with immorality." Coming here in 1794, Mr. Speer preached his first sermon from the text, Eph. 6: 10, "Be strong in the Lord and in the power of His might." Mr. Speer's piety was ardent and self-denying, and his style of preaching most searching and solemn. Fortunately we have, from memoranda kept by himself, the texts and topics of some of these sermons: March 9, 1794, on Mal. 2:15, the Work of the Spirit; May 2, on Rev. 22:17 and Isa. 55:11. Mr. Speer preached occasionally at Great Cove, Greencastle, Bedford, Rocky Spring and elsewhere, during this and other years.

June 6 to 8 was Communion week, and on Sabbath, June 8, Mr. Speer was assisted by the Rev. James Lang, his predecessor, in administering the Lord's Supper. At that time there were received on examination, nine; on certificate, six. The total membership was about ninety. This is the first information we have as to membership. The afternoon sermon was from Luke 2: 20, Shepherds glorifying and praising God for all the things that they had heard and seen. On September 28, in the afternoon, he preached to a company of infantry about to march against the Whiskey Rebellion in Western Pennsylvania.

October 8, 1794, Mr. Speer was ordained and installed pastor of this Church. October 11 and 12 General Washington passed through the town on his way to Fort Cumberland.

February 19, 1795, there was a general thanksgiving by appointment of President Washington, on which day Mr. Speer preached on Hos. 11:9. In May following, he was in attendance upon the General Assembly at Philadelphia. May 31 was Communion Sabbath, when there were received five on certificate, two on examination, and *four were refused as unsatisfactory, on examination (!)* His sermon on that day was on John 13:23, The Disciple whom Jesus loved.

November 4, 1795, Mr. Speer was married by the Rev. Dr. John King, at Mercersburg, to Sarah, eldest daughter of Major James Ramsey, merchant. (In passing, it may be be interesting to state that his wife's sister Mary Ramsey was married, October 11, 1798, to Archibald Irwin. They became the parents of Elizabeth, wife of John Scott Harrison, one of whose sons is ex-President Benjamin Harrison. Another sister, Jane F. Ramsey, became the wife of W. H. Harrison, Jr. She presided over the Executive Mansion during the brief presidency of her father-in-law, Wm. Henry Harrison, Sr.)

Mention is made in Mr. Speer's memoranda of sermons on special subjects, June 7, on John 17:21, "That they all may be one, that the world may believe;" July 19 and 26, four sermons on baptism, from Matt. 28: 19–20; Nov. 8, on Luke 14: 10, Christ's lessons from a wedding; October 18, being Communion Sabbath, on Isa. 53.

Nov. 19, 1796, a son, James Ramsey Speer, was born. This son was graduated from Washington College in 1816; began the practice of medicine 1819, and went to Pittsburg 1825. He is represented as a leader in humane and various public enterprises. Died in the ninety-sixth year of his age, September 6, 1891. Two daughters, Mrs. Rev. A. O. Patterson and Mrs. John Riddell were born elsewhere. It is his son William who has furnished us with much of our information.

What this grandson, Dr. Speer, says of Mr. Speer's work in a later charge, is evidently true of his work here. "The texts used reveal the grand centre and the impelling and regulating force of all his teaching and labors,—the grace of the Lord Jesus Christ, the glory of the Lord Jesus Christ, the priceless gift of pardon to us and to the whole world through His blood, the love of the Holy Spirit, and the heavenly riches which He has to bestow, the personal and the world-wide, the spiritual and the material blessings of the Kingdom of God among men." Dr. Speer writes as follows: "A preacher whose sermons and influence were steeped in the spirit of Jonathan Edwards and Whitefield and the Tennents, as you will easily discern from the topics of the sermons already given, would faithfully warn men of their sins while he pointed them to a merciful and omnipotent Redeemer. His sermons, eminently spiritual, and thus distasteful to many who were willing to conform to outward observances but hated truth and admonitions which pierced with the sword of the Spirit, aroused implacable opposition. As even the seraphic Edwards was driven from Northampton, it is not strange that Mr. Speer's ministry at Chambersburg lasted only three years. But the fruits of it in many forms remained and have been a blessing there until this day."

Mr. Speer was released from this charge April 12, 1797, by the Presbytery of Carlisle. His farewell sermon, on Acts 20:17-35, a review of "three years" of labor, was "a solemn and tender admonition, long remembered by some present."

In the following June, Mr. Speer went on a missionary tour to the West and South. October 5 he was dismissed from the Presbytery of Carlisle to that of Transylvania, which embraced parts of Kentucky and Southern Ohio. Coming with some excellent families to Chilicothe, Ohio, (made by Congress, Nov. 3, 1800, the capital of the Northwest Territory,) he established the present Church there, and became the first chaplain of the infant state of Ohio. He also established the church of Mt. Pleasant, Ohio, in the Presbytery of Chilicothe. He took a prominent part in the great revival in Southern Ohio and Kentucky.

Much sickness in his family and domestic afflictions, (the death of a child,) compelled him to leave Chilicothe, and to return to Pennsylvania in November, 1801, for a stay at his old home near Gettysburg, from which place he was invited October 10, 1802, to preach at Greensburg, Pa. He was soon called to the two Churches of Unity and Greensburg, Presbytery of Redstone. The formal acceptance of this call was given in Presbytery, April 19, 1803. From the Fall of 1802 until released from his charge, April 8, 1829, his life was spent in those congregations. He died April 26, 1829. Mr. Speer was the grandfather of the Rev. Wm. Speer, D. D., now of Washington, Pa., who was from 1846-50 a Foreign Missionary and later Secretary of our Board of Education.

Of Mr. Speer's fervent spirit, his intellectual ability, his careful scholarship, his influence in Western Pennsylvania, his interest in educational matters, his share in the removal of the *Presbyterian Banner* to Pittsburg, his great work in developing both Home and Foreign Missionary work, his part in the establishment of the Western Theological Seminary at Alleghany in 1827, and his position as its first Vice President, his efforts to arouse an opposition to the growing power of Free Masonry as then constituted, and his conflict with the infidelity then so powerful in his region, and above all, his intense and untiring zeal in the "Great Revival of 1800" and in subsequent revivals, of all these an account is given in a most interesting sketch of his life on pages 37-54, in the volume recounting the Centennial Celebration of the Greensburg (Pa.) Church, on April 14-17, 1888, a copy of which volume is herewith presented to our Church by Mr. Speer's grandson, the Rev. William Speer, D. D., of Washington, Pa.

IV.

REV. DAVID DENNY, 1800 TO 1838.

Permit me to say, in the beginning of this sketch of Mr. Denny's life, that I am especially indebted to two persons who wrote of Mr. Denny from personal knowledge. The extracts given are from their pens. One was the late William C. Lane, M. D., of our town, the other was the late Rev. J. A. Murray, D. D., of Carlisle.

Dr. Murray says "During the second quarter of the last century the Denny family came from the mother country to

Pennsylvania and settled in Chester county. About 1745 the two brothers, William and Walter Denny, removed from Chester to what is now Cumberland county. William lived and died in Carlisle, and had been repeatedly appointed to office by the Supreme Executive Council—in 1768, 1769, &c. He married Agnes Parker, of the valley, and they had two sons and five daughters and hence the Dennys of Pittsburg. Walter settled about two miles south of Carlisle, where he owned a large tract of land. When the Revolutionary War had begun he raised and commanded a company, but was killed at the battle of Crooked Billet (a branch of the Neshamany in Bucks county), when his eldest son, fighting at his side, was captured by the enemy and kept three months on board a Jersey prison ship.. There is a letter in the Pennsylvania Archives, volume 6, page 470, from Brigadier-General Lacey to President Wharton of the Supreme Council giving an account of this battle in May, 1778. Like a true woman Mrs. Mary Denny bravely met the responsibilities of her widowhood and endeavored to discharge lovingly and faithfully a mother's duties to her children, now bereft of their father. Of these she had six, five sons and a daughter.

"Of these David, the subject of this sketch, was the

third in birth order. After suitable preparation he entered Dickinson College, whence he was graduated in 1788, and it was the second class graduated from this time-honored institution. The Rev. Dr. Charles Nesbit was Principal of it, and it was under him also that Mr. Denny studied Divinity. It has been well said, that the sources of the philosophy and the theology at that day were neither so copious nor accessible as at present, and the acquisitions of the students were consequently earned by severer toil and application than the facilities of learning now exact. The lectures of Dr. Nesbit were delivered in such a manner that the members of his class could reduce them to writing as they fell from his lips; and Mr. Denny left several quarto volumes of these lectures, in his own very legible handwriting, and they form a respectable body of metaphysics and theology. Mr. Denny was a great admirer of his distinguished preceptor, and often narrated anecdotes illustrative of his art, learning, and accomplishments."

He was licensed to preach the gospel on October 6, 1791, by the Carlisle Presbytery, and April 9, 1794, was ordained and installed Pastor at Upper Path Valley and Lower Path Valley, where he continued until October 9, 1800, in the enjoyment of the esteem and affection of a much loved people. November 24, 1800, he was installed Pastor of the Falling Spring Church, which he retained until the termination of his public ministrations, April 11, 1838, when he was released by the Presbytery. He died December 16, 1845.

"For a period of 38 years Mr. Denny carefully watched over the interests of his people. Our earliest recollections of religious worship," (wrote Dr. Lane in 1851,) "are associated with this faithful minister and his handsome Church. Many a weary Sabbath hour of our childhood was passed within those Church walls, listening to the message of the venerable man, which our youthful mind could not comprehend. We were taken there by kind and endeared friends, now, alas! no more. In imagination, we can yet see the man of God, with his locks silvered by the snows of many winters, delivering his message of love to his attentive hearers, and urging them to accept the salvation purchased by the blood of the Redeemer, which he, as His special ambassador, was empowered to offer them. We can yet see the familiar form of our old teacher, Mr. Blood, as he stands in front of the congregation, to raise the song of praise. We see, too, the faces of many of our old citizens, then members of the congregation, who with their beloved Pastor, are now realizing in the heavenly world, that 'it is no vain thing to serve the Lord.' Mr. Denny was, in all respects, a faithful shepherd, and watched with zealous care, over the spiritual welfare of his flock. Under his ministry, were brought up many of the most consistent and worthy Christians of our town, and they will unite with us, in a feeble attempt to commemorate the exalted worth of their aged and revered friend and Pastor. * * He was a man of commanding intellect, deeply versed in theology, and possessing a classic and cultivated taste, enriched by his extensive acquaintance with the polished productions of Greece and Rome, with which his vocation as teacher for many years made him familiar. Yet he was humble and unaffected; and his mild and courteous deportment pointed to one who had deeply imbided the lovely virtues of his Divine Master. To the young he was especially devoted; and in eloquent, persuasive tones, often warned them to forsake the devious paths of sin, and walk in the narrow, yet peaceful path of wisdom, which eventually leads to ineffable delights in the heavenly world. To the poor and illiterate, as well as to the cultivated and opulent, his ear was always open, and the burdened heart never was unlocked in vain, but always departed soothed by the kind assurance of sympathy and the consolations of Christianity, which he was so well able to impart. During his long connection with the Church, his prominent desire was to advance the spiritual welfare of his congregation; and his long life was a lovely exemplification of the hallowing effects of the Religion of Jesus Christ. Of him we may truthfully say,

> 'He sought not praise, and praise did overlook
> His unobtrusive merit; but his life,
> Sweet to himself, was exercised in good
> That shall survive his name and memory.'

"While pastor in Chambersburg, and during a series of years, he served faithfully and acceptably as teacher of the learned languages in an academy in the place; and many a youth was inspired with a love of knowledge under his capable instruction, and all the better prepared for his subsequent career and life work." (Dr. Murray.)

There still remains a part of the old orchard, (now on the property occupied by Mrs. M. S. King, at Third and Market Streets,) then the property of Mr. Denny, from which, says Dr. Lane, "we schoolboys often filled our pockets with the 'forbidden fruit.'"

Mr. Denny was very happily married, July 25, 1793, to Margaret Lyon, eldest daughter of William Lyon by his second wife, Ann Fleming, of Carlisle, Pa. She died about the time of his retirement from his ministry. "She was a lady of superior worth, and fond partner of his pilgrimage." Dr. Murray concludes his notice of Mr. Denny in the following appreciative words:

"It has been truthfully and beautifully said of him, that his person, cast in the finest mold for strength, activity and symmetry, was well adapted to the air of dignity which nature herself had impressed upon it. His mind was of a strong and discerning order, always governed by candor and sincerity, and warmed by the love of truth. His views were expressed in the language of simplicity and earnestness neither adorned nor obscured by the garnish of imagery or the flashes of rhetoric. He was a decided Calvinist, and conscientiously attached to the standards of the Presbyterian Church. Modesty and humility were interwoven with the very texture of his heart, and its liveliest sympathies were always in expansion for the sick, the suffering, and the desolate. Neither inclemency of weather nor transient illness were suffered to detain him from the exercises of the pulpit, and he enjoyed, in no ordinary degree, the esteem and affection of the people among whom he had so long labored. He was actuated in social intercourse by a manly, tolerant and liberal spirit, that was alike enjoyable, improving, and elevating. He was an honored man, whose life and character could not but have both a present and future power for good upon the community where he spent his ministry. It could not be otherwise, as he left to all who stood in private and public relations to him, an example of sterling virtues, which they can never cease to admire, and whose moulding influence is perpetual. In addition to his active interest in other Christian enterprises, he took a prominent part in the formation of "The Franklin County Bible Society," *which was organized in Chambersburg, December 12, 1814—three years before the American Bible Society was founded—and it embraced some of the very best men of the county, clergy and laity, among its officers and members."

In the History of Carlisle Presbytery, we read of Mr. Denny, that "he was a man possessed of talents of a high order, and had a well-balanced mind, and his was a character distinguished for great excellence. He was a sincere

---

*There is a notice in the Chambersburg *Repository* of July, 15, 1815, of a sermon preached by the Rev. John Lind before this Society.

and ardent lover of truth, and always open and candid in the expression of his views. His style of preaching was noted for its simplicity and earnestness, rather than for rhetorical finish and ornament. Modesty and humility were inherent traits of his character, and he was tender and sympathetic in his feelings for the sick and the afflicted, the poor and the suffering."

During Mr. Denny's time, the Sabbath School was founded about 1816, a history of which will be given this evening.

Mr. Denny left seven sons and three daughters, one of whom became the wife of the Hon. Nathaniel Ewing, of Uniontown, Pa. This lady's granddaughter is the wife of Prof. J. J. Stevenson, of New York City. Two other daughters of Mr. Denny resided here until they died, not many years ago, leaving a memory fragrant with good works. A sister of Mrs. Denny, Miss Alice Lyon, became the wife of the Hon. George Chambers. Her descendants are with us to-day.

The Assembly's Minutes for 1825, the first year in which statistics are given in detail, show that during that year, the membership was 110, that 52 infants were baptised, and seven adults; that $15.00 were given to Foreign Missions, and $13.00 to Theological Seminaries.

But one member now remains on our Church roll of those who were received into the Church during those years, Mrs. Jane Senseney, who was received May, 1838, just a month after Mr. Denny was released from this charge by Presbytery.

V.

REV. WILLIAM ADAM, 1840 TO 1841.

Mr. Adam was born in Glasgow, Scotland, May 15, 1800, being the son of John and Agnes Minto Adam, and a descendent of the elder son of Sir Gilbert Elliot Minto, later

Lord Minto, well-known as a statesmen of ability and eminence in Great Britain from 1774 to 1814. Mr. Adam early united with the Relief Presbyterian congregation of Anderston, Glasgow. His boyhood's Pastor, the Rev. Gaven Struthers, D. D., wrote, on the occasion of Mr. Adam's coming to America, that he had been a lad of highly respectable attainments and of irreproachable character. And the Rev. James Thomson, D. D., the Professor of Sacred Theology in the Relief Divinity Hall, wrote at the same time that Mr. Adam had maintained an excellent character from his earliest years. His application to the studies preparatory for the ministry was the result of his own choice. He received his education in the Languages and Philosophy in the University of Glasgow. While there he received a medal "for superior merit in the Junior Mathematical Class, 1823".* He entered the Relief Divinity Hall in August, 1825, and attended lectures there for four successive sessions, where he showed himself to be a young man of good abilities. Dr. Thomson "was much pleased with his piety, diligence and progress in his studies." Dr. Thomson some years after that, April 18, 1838, recommended Mr. Adam to American Presbyterians "as a man of unblemished reputation, sound in the faith, apt to teach, and a highly useful and acceptable preacher of the Gospel." He had a long period of probation, but for two and a half years he was off the List of Preachers, and seems to have been out of connection with the Relief Church. On October 7, 1834, he was received back at his own request to communion and to his place as a Probationer. August 27, 1837, Mr. Adam was ordained and installed by the Relief Presbytery of Dumfries, as Pastor of the Relief Presbyterian Church of Dumfries, on which occasion the Rev. Archibald Tudehope, of Annan, known to some in our

---

*This medal may be seen in the Chapel.

church as having come to America with Mr. Adam, and later Pastor of the Ninth Church, Philadelphia, "stated the progress of events, proposed the usual questions, and ordained."* (It may be mentioned in passing that the Relief Presbytery and Synod of Scotland, which seceded from the Established Church in 1752, held the doctrines of the Westminster Confession of Faith, with the exception of the chapters relating to the power of the magistrate in religious matters. In 1847 it united itself with the Associate Church, thus forming what has since been known as the United Presbyterian Church of Scotland.)

Another reason given by Mr. Adam for desiring to be released was that he had long cherished a desire to come to America, regarding it as a field of usefulness more suited to his abilities, and he felt that the time had come when this hope could be gratified.

The Rev. Robert Small, D. D., of Edinburgh, thus writes: Dumfries congregation had been greatly injured by Mr. Adam's predecessor going over to the Established Church, and taking a good part of the people with him. The stipend promised Mr. Adam was £80, with £2 at each communion and the possession of the Manse at the following Whitsunday. But before Whitsunday came Mr. Adam tendered his resignation, March 13, 1838. He had lost all hopes of doing good in Dumfries, and believed that the interests of the Relief Church there would be promoted by the induction of another minister. The congregation in reply complained that he had not given Dumfries a long enough trial, that he had not tested his abilities in the way of visiting those who were under his ministry or friendly disposed to the Relief cause, while they stated that his labors among them had been very highly esteemed and appreciated. They could not understand how their

---

*Extract from Minutes of Relief Presbytery of Dumfries, attested, April 19, 1838, by Henry Patterson, Presbytery Clerk.

interests could be promoted when he was throwing them into the greatest confusion. This was at a meeting held April 3, 1838. They left the matter in the hands of the Presbytery, and the Presbytery that day "loosed Mr. Adam from his charge, and agreed to give him a ministerial certificate."

Just before leaving his Dumfries charge, the following paper was adopted by his Church and congregation: "Our esteemed Pastor, the Rev. William Adam, being about to leave this country for America, we cannot allow him to depart without expressing our unqualified approbation of him as a man, a Christian, and a minister. He came among us with a character unspotted as a man, serious as a Christian, and eminent as a preacher, and he leaves us with the same high character. Under his ministry we progressed much externally, and we trust also internally. Consequently his departure from among us is a matter of deep sorrow and regret. We earnestly wished his continuance with us, and did everything in our power to retain him. But having set his affections on America, and looking on it as a better and more extensive sphere of Christian usefulness, we could not prevail upon him to comply with our ardent wishes. Our prayers attend him, and we feel assured that go where he may he shall prove himself a diligent, a faithful, and an acceptable minister of Jesus Christ.

Signed in name and by authority of the Session. } THOMAS MOFFAT, Clerk. JAMES WELSH, Elder.

Signed in name and by authority of the Managers.* } THOMAS DOBBIE, Preses. DAVID REDMOND, Treas.

Relief Church, Dumfries, 28th March, 1838."

At the time of his release from his charge, April 3, 1838, his Presbytery adopted the following: "At the date hereof, the Rev. Mr. Adam, to the surprise and grief of all the Brethren, having from conscientious motives, formally ten-

---
* Trustees.

dered his resignation of the charge of his congregation, and given reasons for so doing, still petitioned that his demission might be accepted.

"The Presbytery did therefore, with deep regret, entertain the above application, and dissolve the pastoral relations subsisting between him and his people; but, at the same time, gladly embrace the opportunity of bearing testimony to the unblemished moral and religious character and deportment of their respected brother; to his evangelical and Scriptural views of divine things; and to his zeal and fidelity in the work of the ministry, for the good of immortal souls."

The Rev. Alex. Neilson, Minister of the Relief Church, Carluke, also testified that Mr. Adam was "possessed of all the qualities which constitute the gentleman, and the higher qualities which form the Christian. No one," adds Mr. Neilson, "I believe, has ever left the religious denomination to which I belong with more ardent admirers of his character, and I doubt not but that he will secure friends as affectionately attached to him, wherever he may go."

The Rev. R. Wilson, minister of the Partick Relief Church near Glasgow, wrote of him, among other things: "As to the vigorous and faithful discharge of Pastoral duties, there are none in whom I could repose greater confidence."

The Rev. Gaven Struthers, already quoted, wrote: "Mr. Adam quits his native country without a stain. The breath of suspicion has never breathed upon his reputation. He is universally esteemed as a Christian minister. He has much of the spirit of his Master, and all his discourses are not only tasteful and well constructed, but full of unction, sweetness and winning appeals."

It is not surprising that on such testimonials as I have quoted from, Mr. Adam was readily received under the care of the Presbytery of Carlisle, when he presented his dismissal from the Relief Presbytery of Dumfries, October 2 and 3, 1839. As is the custom with ministers coming from other bodies, he was examined on Experimental Religion, Theology, Ecclesiastical History and Church Government, and he having signified his approval of the Standards of our Church, his examination was sustained.

Meanwhile, early in 1839, Mr. Adam began to supply the pulpit of this Church. He was appointed by Presbytery to preach the opening sermon at its session in Carlisle, on the second Tuesday in April, 1839. On the 26th of September he was called to be Pastor of this Church, at a salary of "eight hundred dollars per annum, in regular half-yearly payments, on the first Mondays of April and October."* He continued to supply the pulpit from September 1839 until May 2, 1840, when he was regularly installed Pastor. He was released from this charge, April 13, 1841, being compelled to resign on account of a serious throat trouble. On that same day he was dismissed to the Presbytery of Huntingdon. He then went back to Scotland for a visit, returning somewhat improved in health. He was received by the Presbytery of Huntingdon, May 24, 1842, and accepted calls to the Churches of Sinking Creek and Spring Creek, in Penn's Valley, Centre Co., Pa. He was installed there May 25, 1842. He was released from that charge October 7, 1845, and given permission to labor outside the Presbytery. He was dismissed to the Presbytery of Baltimore, April 8, 1851, but there is no record of his having presented his letter to that Presbytery.

Mr. Adam's voice failed him for many years previous to his death, which obliged him to give up preaching. He then opened a book-store on Pennsylvania Ave., Washington, D. C., where he sold only books of a religious nature. He attended the New York Ave. Church for many years, and later connected himself with the Central Church, be-

---

*From the original call in the possession of Mr. Adam's heirs.

longing to the Southern Presbyterian Church, whose Pastor was and still is the Rev. A. W. Pitzer, D. D.

An intimate friend of Mr. Adam's, Mr. William Ballantyne of Washington, D. C., writes that in the year 1852 Mr. Adam kept the book-store above mentioned on Pennsylvania Avenue, and attended the same church with Mr. Ballantyne. "After a few years he retired from business, having accumulated a moderate fortune. His health was always poor. He lived in comfort, but very quietly, and was most regular in his habits. For years before his death no one was more regular in his attendance upon the Daily Prayer Meeting. He made but few friends, and those he had were very dear. Having never married, he boarded in a private family. When on his death-bed he was attended by a sister who lived in Norfolk, Va." He also left a brother, Mr. Richard Adam, of Richmond, Va., to whose widow we are greatly indebted for much information.

He is described by those here who remember him, as a man of social nature, and as a most gifted sermonizer.

Toward the end of Mr. Adam's life he suffered much from heart disease and a complication of troubles that rendered him an invalid for several years. He died in Washington, D. C., July 28, 1883. His remains were taken to Richmond, Va., by a special request made to his brother some years previous, and now side by side the two brothers rest in the beautiful Hollywood Cemetery.

I close this sketch of Mr. Adam with a brief statement made by himself in May, 1876. "Having on the fifteenth day of this month entered upon the seventy-seventh year of my life, and believing that I cannot much longer be a sojourner here below, I desire to state to you my prospects for another. I trust and believe there is a better world beyond the grave. And here at the commencement of this communication I would state clearly and explicitly that I have no hope in myself or in any thing I have done or can do as the ground of my salvation and acceptance with God. I believe that a man can no more redeem himself than he can create himself; that self-salvation is just as impossible as self-creation; that the one is as much beyond the power of man as the other; that consequently both are dependent upon God. It is upon God, therefore, through the great Redeemer, that I look for salvation. There is none other name given under heaven or amongst men whereby sinners can be saved. This alone I believe is solid as well as Scriptural ground on which to stand, as the following passages of Scripture most clearly declare: John 1: 11–13; Gal. 3: 26; 1 John 5: 1; Rom. 10: 9."

Mrs. McElroy Shively, of Scotland, is the only member left on our roll of those who were received into our Church during Mr. Adam's pastorate.

VI.

REV. DANIEL M'KINLEY, D. D., 1841 TO 1850.

Dr. McKinley was born in Carlisle, in the fall of 1801. Living with his widowed mother in the country, when only eight years old he went out alone into a field, and kneeling down, prayerfully and deliberately gave himself to God, to be used by Him, in whatever way would most redound to His glory. His boyhood was wellnigh blameless. He was known among his fellows as the peace-maker, and when not successful in his efforts would leave the scene of conflict. His mother seldom, if ever, had cause to reprove him, and could well say he never caused her a single heartache. He early united with the First Presbyterian Church of Carlisle, under the pastoral care of the Rev. Dr. Geo. Duffield. His piety was so marked and his talents so promising, that Dr. Duffield advised his studying for the ministry. He entered Dickinson College, and was graduated therefrom in 1824 under the presidency of the Rev. Dr. John M. Mason.

The history of the Presbytery of Carlisle contains in part the following sketch of Dr. McKinley:

"From the beginning of his religious life he was a great lover of ministers, missionaries and the cause of missions, and the burden of his prayers was that God would raise up and send forth more laborers into the harvest. During his course in Dickinson College, that extensive revival of religion took place, which arose in connection with the death and funeral services of the son of Dr. John M. Mason, and which pervaded the College and the Church at that time and in the promotion of which young McKinley took an active and most efficient part, and whose efforts, in connection with this work, were untiring and most valuable. Dr. Duffield is known to have referred frequently to his labors at this time, and to have remarked that he had rarely or never known one of his years so competent and successful in the matter of directing inquiring souls to the Saviour."

He took a full course at Princeton Seminary, and was licensed by the Presbytery of Carlisle, September 29, 1826. On October 30, 1827, he was ordained and installed Pastor of the Presbyterian Church at Bedford, Pa., Dr. Duffield preaching the ordination sermon. He remained at Bedford until he was released by Presbytery, September 28, 1831. "In this Church he labored earnestly and successfully for four years, when he was compelled, by reason of the development of a bronchial affection, which proved to be the plague of all his after life, to seek a dissolution of his pastoral relation and to desist from ministerial duties for a period of about two years. The church at Bedford, while not blessed with any special season of grace, was steadily strengthened and built up under his faithful and zealous ministry, and he became greatly endeared to the people as their Pastor, and it was with the deepest reluctance that they yielded to the necessity for the dissolution of the pastoral relation.

"It was at this time, in 1833, that the Second Presbyterian Church in Carlisle was organized. The attention of this people was at once turned to Mr. McKinley, and as he had become encouraged by the improved state of his health, a call was made out for his services, which he accepted, and was duly installed Pastor of this Church on August 7, 1833, and remained until July 31, 1838." Among the eldership were several who had been his Sabbath School teachers. In this reversal of positions, they never failed to accord him full honor and devotion. Here as elsewhere he was regarded with peculiar love by the young. They recognized how much he had their good at heart, how earnestly he longed to see them "remember their Creator in the days of their youth," and they often of their own accord sought his counsel and help. Many still living can rise up and call him blessed, while many more now join with him in the new song sung around the throne of the Lamb. In the sick chamber his sympathy and prayers always brought comfort to the sufferer. In the inquiry room the Holy Spirit so inspired his words and prayers that many were won to make choice of the Saviour. "He continued in this relationship for about five years. His ministry was earnest, zealous and eminently successful. Special seasons of religious interest occurred at different intervals, and during his pastorate of five years seventy-six were added to the Church on profession of their faith. The Church had become firmly established under his ministry, and he left it in a healthy and prosperous condition, having greatly endeared himself to the people, and won the respect and confidence of all classes in the community.

"It was at this time that the Board of Foreign Missions was organized, and efforts were then being made to arouse the Churches to a liberal and general support of this agency of the church for the evangelization of the heathen world, and Mr. McKinley, on account of his known zeal in the missionary cause, and general fitness for the work, was selected as the person to act as general agent and was urged accept the appointment. This he consented to do, and was released from his pastoral charge accordingly, on July 31, 1838, and for more than three years, (until 1841,) he plead the cause of Foreign Missions with great zeal, earnestness and success. His efforts in this connection contributed greatly to the advancement of the cause and made a deep and lasting impression upon the Churches of his own Presbytery as well as the Church at large. He laid special emphasis upon the duty of professing Christians laying aside every week, according as the Lord had prospered them, and of contributing systematically a certain proportion of their income to the cause of Christ. He became thus one of the pioneers in the matter of systematic beneficence.

"In the fall of 1841, Dr. McKinley was called to become the Pastor of the Falling-Spring Church, which call he accepted, was installed November 5, 1841, and continued in charge of the same for about nine years. He returned to the pastoral work with great zeal and earnestness. He was a faithful and pungent preacher of the gospel, and an affectionate and devoted Pastor. In about a year after his installation a gracious and powerful revival of religion took place in the congregation, the results of which were permanent and most salutary in the Church and community. At the ensuing communion thirty-two were added to the Church on profession of their faith, and a great impulse was given to vital religion in the congregation. His pastorate in this Church was eminently faithful and successful, and during the nine years of its continuance, one hundred and four were added to the church on profession of faith."

In 1846, he was very instrumental, in connection with the late Robert Black, of Fayetteville, in arresting "the downward tendency" of the work of our Church at Fayetteville. "October 2, 1850, he asked to be released from the Falling Spring Church, [and was dismissed to the Presbytery of Ohio,] in order to take charge of a new enterprise in Pittsburg, the Sixth Church, and one which it was thought would be a field for which he had special adaptedness. In this, however, his expectations and those of his friends were not fully realized. Owing to the general discouragements incident to new organizations, at the end of the first year's labors there, he asked to be released and returned again to the Presbytery of Carlisle, October 22, 1852.

"The Church at Middletown had been recently organized, and the Presbytery enlisted the services of Mr. McKinley in its behalf, and he was induced to visit the Churches and solicit aid for its establishment, and, by reason of his personal ministry in that congregation and the contributions he secured for its advancement, that Church gave promise of soon becoming one of the self-sustaining congregations of the Presbytery. This expectation however failed to be realized, and largely it is believed for want of unity of feeling and co-operation upon the part of some of its officers and members.

"After spending a year in this service Dr. McKinley was induced to become agent and itinerant missionary for the Board of Home Missions. This was a two-fold work for which he had special qualifications, had his health been sufficient for its earnest and vigorous prosecution. As it was the Board, with melancholy pleasure, bore their united and recorded testimony to his eminent piety, zeal and usefulness, as one of their most efficient and devoted agents, as he had been previously a devoted and useful Pastor.

"His zealous labors as an evangelist and as an agent for the Board, together with the exposure to which he was continually subject, in a short time developed and brought on again with increased severity, his old bronchial trouble.

"In this, his last sphere of ministerial labor, he was, however, instrumental of great good. He knew not how to spare himself when seasons of spiritual awakening in the Churches took place. He was active and zealous in a number of extensive revivals of religion in several of the Presbyteries of the Synod of Philadelphia, especially in the churches of Waynesboro, Newton Hamilton, Sinking and Spring Creek, Lower Tuscarora, Lewistown and other Churches of Huntingdon Presbytery, and also in a number of churches in Donegal and New Castle Presbyteries. In these revival scenes he took great interest. He was always, in every sphere of ministerial labor, zealous and active, and always exerting himself beyond his strength, but in these revival scenes he was unwilling to desist whilst there was any evidence of the special presence and saving efficacy of God's Spirit. He was very kind, and attentive, and attractive to inquiring souls, and greatly blessed in directing them into the way of peace and holiness. His services at such times were always eagerly sought and highly prized by his brethren and greatly enjoyed by the people.

"In the spring of 1855, by reason of his arduous labors of the preceding winter, and on account of the return of his old bronchial affection, aggravated by other painful and serious maladies, his health, under the progress of his disease, which baffled the best medical skill, steadily declined during the summer. His bronchial affection during the later stages of his sickness, almost entirely prevented his engaging in conversation. But through all his sickness and suffering he gave unmistakable evidence of resignation, and faith, and hope, and his last end was peace. He had gone to Chambersburg in the hope of being able to attend the meeting of the Synod of Baltimore, which was to convene there in October, but here, by reason of his rapid decline, he was detained to die, and to enter upon his eternal rest, and the enjoyment of his gracious and glorious reward." He died on his birthday, December 7, 1855.

"Dr. McKinley was a man whose heart, all his life long, was thoroughly enlisted in the great work of extending Christ's kingdom. He was a man of eminent piety, and of a pure and consecrated life." "He gave every evidence of a truly good man, according to the high standard of the Christian calling. In all places wherever he was known, among saints and sinners, there has been but one opinion as to the depth and fervor of his piety—a piety which evinced itself in very early youth. He was kind, affectionate and attractive in aspect and address. He had large views of the duties of the Church, and of society."

"He was in his day a practical and pungent preacher of the gospel, a zealous and ardent advocate of the cause of missions, both home and foreign. He was a firm believer in revivals of religion, and labored and prayed that he might be instrumental in their promotion. In every depártment of ministerial labor in which he engaged, he generally had the seal and approval which comes from the blessing of God." To the very close of his life, his services were in demand wherever there were indications of a revival. A brother minister remarked that his course through Carlisle Presbytery as well as other Presbyteries could be traced not only by increased gifts but by a large harvest of souls.

In 1844, this Church had enrolled 130 communicants, and in 1850, this number had grown to 170.

Dr. McKinley's remains lie buried in the old graveyard at Carlisle, under a stone erected to his memory by the members of the Falling Spring Church.

"On May 31, 1827, he was united in marriage to Miss Mary Wyeth, of Harrisburg, Pa., who died January 15, 1892. By her he had two daughters, one, the intelligent and accomplished wife of the Rev. James F. Kennedy, D. D., the other died in early childhood."

VII.

REV. JOSEPH CLARK, 1852 TO 1857.

For the facts about Mr. Clark I am mainly indebted to notices published at the time of his death.

Mr. Clark was born near Carlisle, Pa., October 11, 1825. He was a lineal descendant of Joseph and Margaret Clark, Scotch–Irish Presbyterians, who came to this country from Ireland in 1739, and settled in the vicinity of Carlisle. Robert Clark, the grandson of Joseph, was twice married. By his second wife there were three sons, the oldest of whom was the Rev. Joseph Clark, the subject of this sketch. He had the advantage of being reared in a Christian family, and at the early age of sixteen united with the Second Presbyterian Church in Carlisle, then under the pastoral care of the Rev. T. V. Moore, and where his father was a Ruling Elder. He received his preparatory education in New Bloomfield, Perry County, Pa., where he soon declared his intention to study for the ministry. He entered Marshall College, then at Mercersburg, Pa., in 1845, whence he was graduated in September, 1848, with the highest honors of his class, delivering the "Marshall Oration." From Mercersburg he went to Allegheny, and was graduated from the Western Theological Seminary in the spring of 1851. On June 11, 1851, he was licensed by the Presbytery of Carlisle. Soon after

this (September 14, 1851,) he was invited to fill the pulpit of the Falling Spring Church, and so acceptable were his services to the congregation that they soon tendered him a call. June 3, 1852, he was ordained and installed as pastor. He discharged his duties with great acceptance until October 7, 1857, when he was released by Presbytery, in consequence of a disease of the throat which rendered it hazardous for him to continue longer in the practice of public speaking. It is said that before he could be induced to relinquish his work as a minister, even upon eminent medical advice, his disease had become so violent that he was frequently obliged to stop in the midst of a discourse and leave it unfinished, as it would have endangered his life to have proceeded any further.

Mr. Clark then sought to recruit his shattered health and gain a livelihood by engaging in a mechanical pursuit. He erected and managed a planing mill, showing the same spirit of enterprise and energy as formerly he did in his ministerial work. Though out of real sympathy with this secular work, and regarding it as a providential necessity, he sought to be satisfied with it, doing what he had found to do with his might, and continued in the active prosecution of his business until the week of his death. Whenever his strength permitted, and he was called upon to do so, he preached the Word. With improved general health Mr. Clark longed to return to the direct employment of his mental gifts in the service of Christ. He could hardly hope to sustain the tax and strain of regular preaching and pastoral work. He therefore conceived the idea of establishing a Theological and Scientific Review for the defence and promulgation of truth. He planned and prayed, he labored and talked and wrote in the interest of such a journal. But all in vain. For his apparently premature death brought all those plans to an end.

Almost the last work of his life was to prepare an address for the national day of humiliation and fasting,—an address which it was not permitted him to deliver, for the hand that penned it was soon after crushed, and the voice that was to have delivered it was hushed in death. He met with a painful accident, Monday, June 5, 1865, and on the following Friday, June 9, death came, unexpectedly to all, even to himself. On the following Sabbath morning, impressive funeral services were held in this Church, on which occasion the Revs. B. S. Schneck, I. N. Hays, and W. A. West paid fitting and touching tribute to the memory of their departed brother.

Mr. Clark's death was a loss not fully measurable, to the Church, and to the world of letters as well. When a boy he gave evidence of great and diversified talents. Even as an under-graduate he was counted a brilliant essayist. He was thorough, not merely in some, but in all the branches of study in the college course. The ease with which he gained and retained and used knowledge, gave him a reputation both with fellow-students and professors. His reading and study embraced books outside those used in the course, and he frequently wandered off into broader fields of science, literature, and art. His mind, vigorous and well-trained, digested and held available what he learned. Thus he could "bring out of his treasures things new and old." His mind has been characterized as one of uncommon power and originality, and of fearless independence of thought and action. Those who listened to his preaching describe his sermons as being "solid as granite and clear as a block of ice," full of earnest logical thought, and fresh and interesting treatment, occasionally breaking out into a strain of rugged, peculiar eloquence which had a charm all its own. And Mr. Clark not only preached many good sermons; he made addresses before literary institutions, and furnished learned criticisms and brilliant essays for the most prominent reviews and journals of the land, winning the highest praises from the wise men of his day. He delighted to grapple with abstruse theories and doctrines. In some of his investigations he startled what he was pleased to call "the orthodox camp," by the boldness and originality of his views. Yet in all his speculations, such as men who think for themselves must at times indulge in, there were visible evidences of strong religious convictions and abiding faith in the truth of God's Word. Yet, while firm and fearless when he felt he was right, there was a certain modesty that made him shrink from making himself conspicuous.

The following is a partial list of some of his publications: in the *Princeton Review* of 1862, one article on "The History and Theory of Revolutions;" and in 1863, one on "The Skepticism of Science," both of which attracted considerable attention at the time; in the Mercersburg *Review*: Bailey's Festus, Eureka, Persecution of Philosophy, Francis Jeffrey, The Strong Character, Some of Our Popular Amusements, Two Funerals, Conybeare's Life of St. Paul, Conybeare's Epistles of St. Paul, Historical Pretensions of Free Masonry, Chief Justice Gibson, Hugh Miller, Hugh Miller as a Geologist.*

Those who knew Mr. Clark describe him as gentlemanly in all his deportment, and kind in all his relations to his fellowmen. He never seemed vain of his superior talents and learning, nor uncharitable to others. His ill health did not make him irritable or impatient. While an earnest thinker, he was not morose. He was reserved without being cold. In the circle of his familiars, he was exceedingly companionable and pleasant.

As a Christian, he realized that without saving faith, there could be no strong, symmetrical character. Without this, talent and genius are either dangerous or perverted gifts, or both. And with him, greatness and goodness could be united only in the man of strong head and pure heart, both renewed by the Holy Ghost.

Mr. Clark's heart was in this Church, his first and only charge. He sought its welfare in every possible way. He lent his skillful hand and active brain. The Church was enlarged during his ministry by adding to its front the vestibules and several feet to its length. Mr. Clark himself was so eager and interested in this, that he used the hammer upon many a stone. To him also we are indebted for the

---

*This list is secured through the kindness of the Rev. W. C. Cremer, of our town.

only roll of the then members now extant, he having prepared it with as great accuracy as he could from incomplete data in his hands. Mr. Clark prefixed the following note to the register of communicants: "It is very much to be regretted that this Register must necessarily be so imperfect. As was customary in many of the old Churches of this region, the records of this Church in its early days were kept in so loose and temporary a form that they soon became scattered and lost. The records of Presbytery show that the organization of Falling Spring Church took place shortly previous to the year 1739. From the time of its organization not a trace of its communicant members is now to be found, until the year 1821. In this way the names of many worthy and pious persons—the pioneers of this region—have been lost to the Church. The present Register begins with 1821, with the list drawn up by the Rev. David Denny, of its then existing members. Of many of these the times of their admission to the Church are not given, nor is it now possible to give the times of their decease or the places of their removal. No Register was kept during the ministry of the Rev. William Adam, 1839 to 1841. The deficiency is very imperfectly supplied from testimony.

"May the Lord add many to this Church 'of such as shall be saved.'

(Signed) "JOSEPH CLARK, Pastor."
"Chambersburg, Pa., October, 1852."

The membership of the Church at the beginning and end of Mr. Clark's pastorate was as follows: in 1852, 193 members; in 1857, 211 members. In 1857, for the first time, special mention is also made of colored communicants, of whom there were in that year three.

VIII.

REV. LAMBERT SUYDAM FINE, 1858 TO 1859.

Mr. Fine was born at Ogdensburg, N. Y., in 1832, and was graduated from Hamilton College, N. Y., in 1854. He took the full three years' course in Princeton Seminary and was graduated therefrom in the spring of 1858. He began to preach here January 5, 1858, was received by the

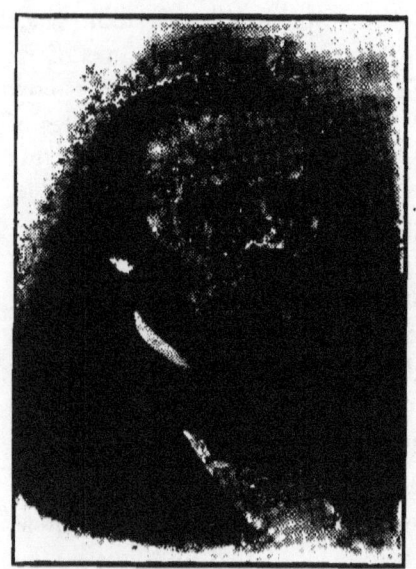

Presbytery of Carlisle, as a licentiate from the Presbytery of Philadelphia, April 14, 1858, and on May 19, 1858, was ordained and installed Pastor of the Falling Spring Church, remaining as its Pastor until released by Presbytery, June 15, 1859. His ministry here ceased October 3, 1859. He was dismissed to the Presbytery of Geneva, N. Y., October 3, 1860. He served the Presbyterian Church at Penn Yan, N. Y., as Stated Supply, during the winter of 1859–60, and until November 21, 1860, when he was received into the Geneva Presbytery by letter from the Presbytery of Carlisle, and installed Pastor of the Church at Penn Yan. He was released from that Church by his Presbytery, June 11, 1861. He supplied for a time the Churches at Sonora, Cal., Liberty, Ohio, and Paris Hill, N. Y., and at Troy, Pa. He died at the last named place, March 5, 1869, of pneumonia brought on by over-exertion at a fire. On June 9, 1868, the Presbytery of Geneva adopted the following resolutions:—"Whereas, the Rev. L. S. Fine, a member of this Presbytery, has, since our last Stated Meeting, been called from this life, we hereby express our humble recognition of the divine hand in this bereavement; our appreciation of his kindly and Christian character, and our thanks to God for this illustration of His recovering and sustaining grace.

"Resolved, That we hereby tender our deep and hearty sympathy to the widow of our departed brother in her great bereavement, and pray that the God of all comfort may ever have her and her orphan children in His blessed and holy keeping."

During Mr. Fine's short pastorate here, he and his family made many dear friends, who cherish the memory to-day of the kindly relations existing between them.

For the years 1858 and 1859 the membership stood at 217. Special mention is also made of colored communicants, two in 1858, and four in 1859.

For the year ending April 1, 1860, during most of which time the pulpit was vacant, the number of communicants reported was 216.

We come now to the pastorates of brethren who are still living, honored and beloved by their friends in this Church and congregation. You will understand the embarrassment of attempting to give more in their presence than the barest outlines of their life and work among us. May the day be long distant when it shall be incumbent upon any one to write more fully and freely of their noble work and faithful labors while here!

IX.

REV. SAMUEL JACK NICCOLLS, D. D., 1860 TO 1864.

Mr. Niccolls was born August 3, 1838, on what is known as the Greenfield Farm, in Westmoreland county, Pa., being the only child of William Todd and Eliza (Jack) Niccolls. His preparatory studies were finished at the Eldersridge Academy, and his college education was completed at Jefferson College, whence he was graduated in 1857. He took the full three years' course at the Western Theological Seminary at Allegheny, Pa., leaving that institution in the spring of 1860. He was licensed to preach by the Presbytery of Redstone in 1859, and in July, 1860, was called to the pastorate of the Falling Spring Church. He commenced his labors here September 14, 1860, was received into the Presbytery of Carlisle, by letter from the Presbytery of Redstone, October 3, and on November 20, was ordained and installed the Pastor of this Church, in which office he remained until released by Presbytery, November 16, 1864, on which day he was also dismissed to the Presbytery of St. Louis, to become Pastor of the Second Presbyterian Church in that city, where he entered upon his ministry in January, 1865. There he still continues, an honored and beloved Pastor, and abundantly blessed in his labors.

Dr. Niccolls' pastorate here covered the greater part of the dark days of the Civil War. During this period, he was granted leave of absence by this Church, that he might serve as Chaplain of the 126th Pennsylvania Volunteers. In this position he remained from September 6 to November 16, 1862, and then returned to his pastoral duties.

Near the end of Dr. Niccolls' pastorate, July 30, 1864, our town was burned by General McCausland, under orders of General Early. Dr. Niccolls has already given us some reminiscences of those terrible days and nights of suffering and loss.

Dr. Niccolls has been the recipient of many honors from the Church at large. He has been prominent in the negotiations between the Northern and Southern Branches of the Presbyterian Church, for the restoration of friendly relations. He was elected Moderator of the General Assembly at Detroit in 1872.

He received the degree of D. D., from Centre College, Ky., in 1867.

The increasing prosperity of our Church during Dr. Niccolls' pastorate, when he so greatly endeared himself to this people, is shown by the increase of membership from 216 to 290. Special mention is also made in the General Assembly's Minutes, of colored communicants, 5 in 1860, and 5 in 1861. After the year 1861, no such special mention is made.

In April, 1865, when the pulpit was vacant, there were reported 267 communicants.

X.

JOSHUA BLACKWOOD HOWELL JANEWAY, PH. D., 1866.

I have succeeded in securing very little in reference to Mr. Janeway's personal history. He was born in Rahway, N. J., May 16, 1837; was graduated from Princeton College,

1857; took the full three years' course in Princeton Seminary, and was graduated thence in the spring of 1861; May 7, 1863, he was ordained and installed by the Presbytery of Raritan, as Pastor of the Amwell First Presbyterian Church, N. J., where he remained through part of the year 1864. He was a Chaplain in the United States Army, from 1864 to 1866. Mr. Janeway supplied this pulpit from January 14, 1866, to September 30, 1866, but never brought his letter to the Presbytery of Carlisle. While here his health, which was seriously injured by his life in the army, was not greatly improved.

On leaving here, Mr. Janeway acted as Stated Supply of the Presbyterian Churches at Pennington, N. J., 1867-68; was pastor of the Second Church, Cranbury, N. J., 1870-75; lived in Trenton, N. J., 1868-70; in Philadelphia, 1870-75; and in 1875 became actuary for the Presbyterian Ministers' Annuity Fund (or Life Insurance Co.), in which position he remained for some years. From Philadelphia he went to Denver, Col., Emporia, Kansas, and San Diego, Cal. He was in 1889 and for some years following a teacher in New York City, where he resides at present. He is a member of the Presbytery of Boulder, Col.

There were reported to Presbytery, April, 1866, 245 communicants, and in April, 1867, 295.

XI.

REV. JOHN AGNEW CRAWFORD, D. D., 1867–1887.

From Nevin's Presbyterian Encyclopædia and other sources we glean the following:

Dr. Crawford is the oldest son of the Rev. S. W. Crawford, D. D., who was born in South Carolina in 1796, and became a distinguished minister of the Reformed Presbyterian Church. Another son was the late General S. Wiley Crawford, well known in connection with the fall of Fort Sumter and the battle of Gettysburg. Dr. Crawford, the father, was successively pastor of Churches of the Reformed Presbyterian denomination in Conococheague, near Chambersburg, and the Second and Fourth Churches in Philadelphia.

He was eminent as an educator, being for many years Principal of the Academical Department of the University of Pennsylvania, as well as Professor in the Theological Seminary of the Reformed Presbyterian Church. He died at Allandale, near Chambersburg, in 1876. His son, the Rev. J. Agnew Crawford, your former Pastor, and our well-beloved and honored friend, was born in Philadelphia in 1822, was educated under his father's care, and entered the University of Pennsylvania, whence he was graduated in 1841. His theological course was taken at the Seminary of the Reformed Presbyterian Church, in Philadelphia. He was licensed to preach by the Reformed Presbytery of Philadelphia, Aug. 15, 1844. In 1847 he was ordained and installed pastor of the Reformed Presbyterian Church at Milton, Pa. He was later on Pastor of the Reformed Presbyterian Churches in Xenia, Ohio, and Brooklyn, N. Y. While in Xenia, Dr. Crawford also taught the languages, and one of his former pupils, the Rev. J. A. Worden, D. D., recently told me that he learned more of the beauty there is in Greek poetry from Dr. Crawford than from any other teacher he ever had.

Dr. Crawford was received by letter from the Reformed Presbyterian Church (North), by the Presbytery of Carlisle, July 9, 1867. On July 10, he was installed Pastor of the Falling Spring Church, in which charge he remained as Pastor until January 1, 1887, when he was released by Presbytery and was made *Pastor Emeritus*, and still continues so to be. For some years he has taught Philosophy and Greek in Wilson College. He has also for many years been Permanent Clerk of the Presbytery of Carlisle. He received the degree of D. D., from the University of Pennsylvania in 1876.

Under Dr. Crawford's long and faithful pastorate this church steadily advanced in numbers, in benevolence, in missionary zeal, and in general efficiency. The Young Ladies' Missionary Society was organized February 21, 1881, under his leadership, and has been persevering and generous in noble deeds and gifts, and is now the banner Band of the Presbytery. The following were the original members, as found in the list given in the Chapel:

Sarah Egery Reed, Sallie Reed, Ellie Chambers, Clara Miller, Jean Agnew Crawford, Susie Monroe Crawford, Annie Chambers, Emma Chambers, Annie M. Linn, Belle

McLellan, Jeannie Senseny, Alice Senseny, Susie Shields Kennedy, Mary Stewart, Lizzie Shumaker, Theodosia Shumaker, Scott King, Nettie King, Elizabeth King, Nellie Lesley, Edith Lesley, Flora Lesley; Rose Hunter, Nellie McIlvaine, Emma Snider, Minnie McDowell, Annie C. McDowell, Clara Scott, Mary Scott, Margery Cain; from Wilson College, Alice Wing, Mary Craig, Margaret Ewalt, Grace Ewalt, Elizabeth Elliot, Kate Elliot, Arianna Kennedy, Anne West, Mollie Eyster, Florence McCullough, Florence Sprecher, Mary Fendrick, Sarah Harris.

This is not the time, nor is this the presence, in which to enter into a more detailed *resume*, or to enlarge more fully upon Dr. Crawford's admirable pastoral work.

June 9, 1871, a number of books published by our Board of Publication were donated by the Sunday School to Wilson College, with the understanding that members of the congregation should have the use of them whenever they desired.

We will hear from others the history of our Sabbath Schools and various Missionary Societies, and of our system of benevolent offerings, and of the formation of the Central Church.

The story of the great revival of 1876-7 was most aptly narrated to us last evening by Dr. Crawford himself.

One of the permanent results of that revival was the organization of the Union Women's Prayer-meeting Jan. 15, 1876, which has to this day been signally blessed of God.

On the opening of the new Chapel, the Session spent much time in prayer that God would bless the chapel study to His own glory and the good of the cause to which that room was consecrated.

. Children's Day was first observed in June, 1886.

The following resolutions were adopted at the congregational meeting which acted upon Dr. Crawford's request to be released from this congregation:

"Whereas our Pastor, Dr. J. A. Crawford, because of

physical inability to meet what he believes to be the requirements of the congregation under present conditions, has tendered a resignation of his pastorate, and has expressed a desire that the congregation unite with him in a request to Presbytery to dissolve the relation which now exists,

"*Resolved*, That the congregation hereby expresses its assent to and acceptance of the resignation of Dr. Crawford, and unites with him in the request to Presbytery for dissolution of the pastoral relation.

"But in doing so we desire further to give expression of our sincere regret for the existence of these conditions which have influenced his action in this regard. For Dr. Crawford this congregation entertains cordial and undiminished affection, esteem and regard, inspired and maintained by his uniform Christian conduct and fellowship and constant faithfulness in his high office, and we recall with grateful recollection the efficient service he has rendered us as a congregation and as individuals thereof.

"*Resolved*, That as a testimonial of our affection and regard for Dr. Crawford, we invite him to become *Pastor Emeritus* of this congregation, and that he be paid an annuity of $300.00 out of the congregational funds, so long as he remains without an active charge."

These resolutions were seconded by Mr. Benj. Chambers, whose address at the time expressed the feelings of the whole congregation toward Dr. Crawford, and their appreciation of his work both as a preacher and pastor. This address and the above resolutions are to be found in full in the Session Records. Remarks were also made at that meeting by Mr. Wm. G. Reed, Rev. John Edgar, John M. McDowell, Esq., John Stewart, Esq., and Geo. Chambers, Esq.

The following statistics speak for themselves, as to our Church's growth in the grace of giving during Dr. Crawford's pastorate: In 1868, the Church contributed to Home

Missions $130.00; in 1886, $728.00. To Foreign Missions $323.00 and $807.00, and to other objects in proportion.*

Of the large number received into the Church during Dr. Crawford's pastorate, there still remain enrolled with us, 51 who were received by letter, and 57 by confession.

Permit me a personal word just here. Dr. Crawford has shown himself to me a kind and ever helpful friend, and I but express the wish of my own heart, and I believe of multitudes in our Church and town, that he may be long spared to dwell among us, and to be cherished by us.

XII.

REV. JOHN GRIER HIBBEN, PH. D., 1887–1891.

Mr. Hibben was born in Peoria, Ill., Apr. 19, 1861. He is the great-great-grandson of the Rev. Robert Cooper, D. D., who came from Ireland and settled in Lancaster Co., Pa., and who was Pastor of the Church at Middle Spring from 1763–1797. Mr. Cooper's second daughter, Elizabeth, married Rev. Isaac Grier, whose third son, John C. Grier was Mr. Hibben's grandfather on his mother's side. Mr. Hibben was graduated from Princeton College, in 1882, entered Princeton Seminary in 1883, and was graduated in 1886. He was licensed by the Presbytery of Peoria, July 2, 1885. He was elected Pastor of this Church at a congregational meeting held Jan. 3, 1887; was received as a licentiate by the Presbytery of Carlisle, April 13, 1887, and was ordained and installed as Pastor, May 19, 1887, remaining in charge until released by Presbytery in April, 1891, having been compelled on account of impaired health to resign, very much to the regret of this people, to whom he had so greatly endeared himself by his faithful and earnest work.

*The Communion Service now in use was given to this Church after the fire, by the First Presbyterian Church of Pittsburg, April 14, 1864.

The following is the minute of the Session meeting Feb. 21, 1891, at which Mr. Hibben first introduced the matter of his resignation of the pastorate here: "All the Elders present expressed their deep sorrow that their beloved friend and Pastor had reached such a decision, and all thought it best that he should remain as long as he felt able and willing. They bore testimony to his faithfulness and success as a pastor, and were unanimous in the opinion that the Church was now more harmonious, stronger, and in better condition than when he assumed the pastorate four years ago."

At the next meeting of the Session, March 2, 1891, it was decided to call a congregational meeting on April 6, 1891, at 3 P. M., to take action upon Mr. Hibben's resignation. At that meeting the following resolutions were unanimously adopted:

"That while we as a congregation deeply deplore the causes that necessitate such a step on the part of our beloved Pastor, yet recognizing that absolute rest is essential to his restoration to health and strength, we reluctantly and sorrowfully accept the resignation tendered, and will join with him in his request to Presbytery to sever the close relations existing between us as Pastor and people. Be it resolved further, that we as a congregation are not satisfied to sever these relations in a mere formal manner, for our Pastor, during his ministry among us, has entwined himself deeply around our hearts and in our lives. The time is fitting and the occasion proper to give expression to the love and esteem in which we hold him, and some recognition of the work he has done in our midst. He has indeed labored faithfully in the vineyard of his Lord and, without stint, has given of his strength to his Master. His daily walk and life were such as to prove his faith to be a living faith and his service a service of a living Christ. Seldom do so many Christian virtues cluster around one character. Noble in purpose, refined in strength, tender and sympathetic in feeling, conscientious in action, charitable toward the weakness of frail humanity, these, ripest fruits of a Christian life are his in marked degree.

"To know our Pastor is to feel that he walks close to his God, and a life that draws its inspiration from this source is an influence for good, not only in the Church, but in the community in which it is spent.

"As a congregation we desire to testify, with gratitude, that God has blessed his labors among us, which is evidenced by the large accessions to the membership of this Church. Though his pastorate has not extended over many years, yet he has started religious activities which now promise blessings to the Church and to advance the kingdom of our Lord and Master Jesus Christ. Recognizing the vital importance of bringing the young early to the Saviour and engaging them in His service, he labored with zeal and success among the youth of the congregation, and awakened in the hearts of many of them the desire to take an active part in the work of the Church.

"The labors of our Pastor were not confined to his own people, but included the community at large, all classes, conditions and colors. Wherever there was need for a minister of God, Mr. Hibben was ready to go. None were too poor, too degraded, but, if they called upon him, he tendered to them his kindly offices. The Chapel in Wolfstown stands as a monument to testify to his love for humanity for humanity's sake.

"Not only his departure, but also, that of his esteemed wife, who has been such an earnest and efficient co-worker in the various avenues of religious work, will be universally regretted. As a congregation, we shall miss his presence from the pulpit; and the community, the benefit of his teachings and his life. Those too whose hearts are weighed down by sorrow, who refuse to be comforted because the grave has closed over all that is mortal of those who, in life, were dear to them, will miss our Pastor. It was when the soul was passing through the troubled waters of affliction, that he was able to bring the sweet consolations and comforting hopes of the Gospel to cheer the grief-stricken soul and to call it back to its allegiance to its Maker, causing it to exclaim through its tears 'Thy will be done.'

"But he shall be missed most of all in the chamber of sickness and of death. He brought with him into the sick room the same faith that was his own guide and comfort in life. He encouraged the suffering to bear with patience their cross, and strengthened the dying to enter without fear the dark valley and shadow, for beyond death and the grave were the rich promises of the Risen Lord.

"The severence of our relations with our Pastor would be sad under any circumstances, but the causes that make this action now a necessity bring with them added sorrow and deep regret. Our hearts go out to him in sympathy in this sore trial, for a trial it is, to be compelled, thus early in his ministry, to suspend his life work. But we know upon whom he leans, and that the support will never fail him, for 'Lo I am with you alway, even unto the end of the world.'

"We shall follow with deep interest his future, and retain

for him a warm place in our affections. We shall remember him in our prayers, that he may soon be restored to health and strength, and again resume the work he is now laying down, a work he loves so well, for it is in the service of his Master. That Master caused the scales to fall from the leper, and said to the dead Lazarus 'Come forth,' and if it is for the best he can heal our Pastor. In the care of Omnipotent Power we leave him."

Mr. Hibben preached his farewell sermon May 24, 1891. He was elected Instructor in Logic and Psychology in Princeton College soon after leaving Chambersburg. He is now Assistant Professor in Logic. In June, 1893, he received the degree of Ph. D. from Princeton College.

During Mr. Hibben's pastorate he was successful in completing the organization of the Wolfstown Mission Sabbath School, about which time the present chapel was built for that school at a cost of $700.00.

The history of the Industrial School connected with this church goes back to the years immediately following the "Fire of 1864." For two years it was in a very flourishing condition, under the care of Mrs. Thos. B. Kennedy and Mrs. Ellen Culbertson, Mrs. M. C. Washington and others. Its meetings were held in the old Lecture Room. After being suspended for a number of years, it was revived and organized June 2, 1890, when a few ladies rented first one room, then two, in Yessel's new brick house at Wolfstown. It met on Mondays, beginning with about half a dozen scholars and four or five teachers. June 18, 1890, the school already registered 80 scholars. Sept. 8, the day was changed to Saturday. When the new Chapel at Wolfstown was opened and dedicated, Dec. 21, 1890, the scholars removed thither, being at the time under the superintendency first of Mrs. Hibben, then of Mrs. Thos. B. Kennedy. Among the ladies then teaching in the school were Mrs.

Alice Grier, Miss Lizzie Wallace, Mrs. Thos. Wallace, Miss Emma Smith, Miss Arie Kennedy, and Mrs. Wm. B. Reed. While in Yessel's building, boys began to attend, and the constant wonder was and is that they prefer the Industrial School to the streets on a Saturday afternoon. The attendance of both sexes, though variable, has been over 100, with about a dozen lady teachers. The object is not to teach fancy work but to do plain and practical sewing, taking special care that the work done be both neat and strong. Flannel is furnished at half-rate to grown scholars. Gingham for aprons is free to all. The smaller scholars are furnished all materials free. Merits are earned by promptness, good behaviour, and careful sewing, and by these merits the scholars purchase the clothing.

The main, underlying purpose of all this work should not be overlooked, namely, the bringing of the scholars, and especially the boys, off the street, and under the sound of the Gospel. To this end, at every session there are hymns, Scripture, prayer, and a short talk upon some intensely practical subject. These influences, under the faithful, energetic, generous efforts of the Superintendent, Mrs. Kennedy, assisted by noble, self-denying teachers, coupled with the School on Sabbath afternoons, by the blessing of God, have resulted in a most marked improvement in many homes, and in the orderliness of the whole neigborhood.

Mr. Hibben also organized in this Church the first Christian Endeavor Society in Franklin Co., which is now so great a help to our young people, and a joy to the present Pastor, and of which Mr. W. B. Reed will give us an account.

During the years of Mr. Hibben's pastorate, the membership increased from 232 in 1887, to 283 in 1891; and the contributions to Foreign Missions from $783.00 to $1051.00.

It is a cause of sincere disappointment to us all not to greet Dr. Hibben at this time. He made a place for himself in the hearts of this people, and he will find that he holds that place today. May the Lord make him as useful and blessed in his present work as he was while Pastor of this beloved Church! We humbly pray for his speedy restoration to health, and long-continued success in his work.

XIII.

REV. HARRIS ROGERS SCHENCK, 1892–

The Rev. H. R. Schenck was born in Philadelphia, Pa., Feb. 27, 1856; was graduated from Princeton College in 1876; taught at the Princeton Preparatory School; entered Princeton Seminary in September, 1877, was graduated, taking a fourth year, and leaving the Seminary in May 1881; was ordained by the Presbytery of Westchester, N. Y., June 7, 1881; was Pastor at Mahopac Falls, N. Y., from 1881–1887; Pastor at Mt. Kisco, N. Y., 1887–1892; was called to the pastorate of the Falling Spring Church, Feb. 9, 1892; was received by the Presbytery of Carlisle, Apr. 13, and installed as Pastor of the Falling Spring Church, May 26, 1892.

NOTE. The Ms. of the above address, which is somewhat fuller than space permitted to print, is on file with other documents belonging to the Church

GREETING FROM THE GREENCASTLE CHURCH,

BY THE REV. L. C. BELL, PASTOR.

On behalf of the Presbyterian Church of Greencastle, I have the honor to present to the Falling Spring Presbyterian Church their heartiest congratulations on your reaching the advanced age of one hundred and sixty years, and the one hundredth as a separate charge. We note with the greatest pleasure that the signs of age, contrary to those of human life, are your increased and increasing strength with all the evidences of buoyant life. We congratulate you upon the able and godly character of those who have stood in your pulpit; upon the representatives of this Church, who have ruled it, and the number and influential character of its membership. We wish that Falling Spring Church may have many more centennials and continue to be a spring of gracious influences, pouring out upon saints and sinners the water of salvation.

The sister church desires to present you, in token of her good wishes, a relic of former days, before the breaking up of the Conococheague church family—a cross made from a piece of wood taken from the "Old Red Meeting House," which stood near "Moss Spring" about three quarters of a mile east of Greencastle. It was built about the year 1767, and used as a church until 1827. The relic is inscribed as follows: "Presented to Falling Spring Presbyterian Church of Chambersburg, Pa., Nov. 12, 1894, by the Presbyterian Church of Greencastle, Pa.," "HO LOGOS HO TOU STAUROV TOIS MEN APOLLUMENOIS MORIA ESTI, TOIS DE SOZOMENOIS HEMIN DUNAMIS THEOU ESTI." (1 Cor. 1: 18).

It is impossible for me to give any personal reminiscences

of the "Lower East Conococheague Church," as my personal knowledge extends over but two years. The pastors, since the time of the separation from the same charge with the "Upper East Conococheague Church," have been, according to records extant, twelve in number, as follows: Rev. Robert Kennedy, Apr. 13, 1803 to Apr. 9, 1816; Rev. James Buchanan, 1816 to Oct. 1, 1839; Rev. Jno. T. M. Davie, Nov., 1840 to Apr. 9, 1845; Rev. T. V. Moore, D. D., Oct. 15, 1845 to Oct. 7, 1847; Rev. Wm. M. Paxton, D. D., Oct. 4, 1848 to Dec. 5, 1850; Rev. Edward Emerson, Sept. 1, 1852 to Aug. 14, 1860; Rev. Wm. T. Beatty, May 16, 1861 to Apr., 1863; Rev. J. W. Wightman, Nov. 12, 1863 to Oct. 4, 1870; Rev. D. K. Richardson, Feb. 10, 1872 to Aug., 1877; Rev. Jas. H. Stewart, Dec. 13, 1877 to May 1, 1883; Rev. J. D. Hunter, Apr. 29, 1884 to May 1, 1892; Rev. L. Carmon Bell, Dec. 20, 1892—.

GREETING FROM THE CENTRAL CHURCH,

BY ELDER W. H. H. MACKEY.

It affords me great pleasure to stand before you to-night to represent the Central Church as a child of the Falling Spring Church. For the reason that the mother has always been very kind to the child, we have under all circumstances felt at perfect liberty to ask any favor we desired, and have appreciated the freeness and kindness with which the favor was granted.

Separations are generally attended with friction, but in this case the separation was similar to a parent's parting with a loved child, going to another part of the country with an object in view for the advancement and welfare of both child and parent. In this case, it was thought better for the advancement of Presbyterianism in our city to separate. I think God's hand was in it, as much as it was in the separation of Paul and Barnabas for the building up of His Church, or in the separation of Joseph from his father for the preservation of the lives of the people. The separation has more than doubled Presbyterianism in Chambersburg. Presbyterianism had had a marked and steady growth in the mother church, until many thought the building too small to accommodate its members; and in the early spring of 1868, when there seemed to be no prospect for a new building, or for an addition to the old one, thirteen of its members prepared a petition favoring a new organization. It was signed by them, and presented to the Presbytery of Carlisle by the Rev. James F. Kennedy, D. D., at a meeting held in Duncannon, June 9, 1868. This petition was considered by Presbytery, and it appointed a committee of three, consisting of the Rev. Thomas Creigh, D. D., the Rev. W. A. West, and Elder J. Craig McLanahan, to visit Chambersburg and organize a second Presbyterian church, if the thought it best to do so.

The committee met in the Falling Spring Church, Aug. 15, 1868, with the pastor, elders and congregation. After a full interchange of views, they decided to organize a second Presbyterian church. The Session of the Falling Spring Church granted certificates of dismissal to twenty-eight of its members, who desired to form the new organization. These certificates being accepted by the committee, the formal organization was accomplished. To complete the organization, an election was held for ruling elders, when James C. Austin and James A. Reside were unanimously chosen to that office.

Six weeks after the organization of this Church, the Rev. Isaac Newton Hays was called to be the first Pastor, and he was installed Dec. 11, 1868. He was released May 5, 1874, to accept a call to Junction City, Kan. The Church was then vacant for three months, when the Rev. John Calvin Caldwell was called, Aug. 3, 1874; and he was installed Oct. 22 following. He was released Aug. 7, 1883, to accept a call to West Chester, Pa. Rev. John Jay Pomeroy was installed as Pastor, April 10, 1884. Dr. Pomeroy continued as our beloved Pastor for a period of five years and eight months, when in the midst of health and vigor he was striken down by an accident, which resulted in his death, Dec. 1, 1889. The present pastor, the Rev. Thomas Johnston Sherrard, was called April 12, 1890, and began his labors here June 1st of that year; he was installed June 10, 1890.

The Church has had, in the course of twenty-six years, four pastors. Beginning with a membership of twenty-eight, at the time of its organization, the congregation increased to one hundred members by the time of the dedication, three years after the organization. It has steadily increased in membership up to the present time. There are now on the roll two hundred and fifty-two names, this being the largest number since the organization.

As a child, and in behalf of the children of the Central Church, I again thank the Mother Church for her kind, cordial and tender nursing through all these years. And above all, we thank the Great Head of the Church for leading and guiding us so safely and so tenderly through the past quarter of a century. May we all ever look to Him for divine guidance; and when the Lord cometh to make up His jewels, may we all be gathered home!

HISTORY OF THE SESSION,

BY DR. G. F. PLATT.

For nearly ninety years of the life of the Falling Spring Church, no permanent record was made either of its officers or private members; hence the names of the worthy men who served in the eldership during those years are lost to us.* In 1821 the Rev. David Denny made a list of the then existing members. The Rev. Joseph Clark in 1852, prepared a Register into which he copied those names, and wherein have been written the names of all who have since joined the Church. In that Register we find the following names of those who were elders at or before that date, and the date of their death or dismissal, but not of their election: Samuel Blood, dismissed to Alleghany, 1839; John Colhoun, died Jan., 1822; Alex. Scott, died Sept., 1822; Joseph Graham, died Aug., 1823; John Lindsay, died Sept., 1825; Andrew McCord, dismissed to Ohio, (no date); Jas. B. Ross, dismissed, 1828; Archibald Fleming, dismissed to Ohio, Mar. 25, 1832; Robert McCracken, dismissed to the west Sept. 14, 1837; John King, died July 8, 1835; Moses Kirkpatrick, died June 6, 1846; Samuel Cooper, died Sept. 28, 1853.

We find the following with date of election as well as death or dismissal. Wm. S. Davis, elected Dec. 3, 1826, died Apr. 24, 1837; David Lytle, elected Dec. 3, 1826, died July 1858; Samuel McElroy, elected Aug. 1843, died Jan. 14, 1855; Robert Sharpe, elected Feb. 3, 1849, died March 11, 1858; Alex. Thompson, elected 1840, died Aug, 2, 1848; Stewart Kennedy, elected Aug. 7, 1843, died March 1, 1852; Robt. Black, elected Sept., 1849, dismissed to Fayetteville, Nov. 27, (no year given).

It is greatly to be regretted that when the town was burned in 1864, the sessional records were all destroyed, hence we have no account of their proceedings prior to that time.

My first remembrance of the ruling elders in this Church was of two gentlemen of hoary locks and solemn mien, walking up and down the aisles, each having in his hand a long rod to the end of which was attached a bag for the re-

*From the fact that the Presbytery Records state that Col. Benj. Chambers on Aug. 31, 1738, "moved to the Presbytery," &c., it would seem that Col Chambers was a member of Presbytery, and therefore a Ruling Elder.—EDITOR.

ception of the weekly gifts of the worshipers. These honored men, Messrs. Holmes Crawford and John Cree, were at that time the only members of Session. Mr. Crawford was of a modest, retiring disposition, so much so that his voice was never heard in prayer or exhortation, either in public or social worship, but he served the Lord with great earnestness, and by the weight of his Christian character commended the religion he professed. He served as clerk until June, 1864, when, pleading the infirmities of age, he asked to be relieved, and at his urgent request his resignation was accepted. About a month after the burning of the town, he took up his abode in the country, and thenceforward was unable to take an active part in the affairs of the Church at home, or to represent the Session in the higher Church Courts. Having "served his own generation" for more than four score years, he "fell on sleep and was gathered to his fathers" in Feb., 1874. He was elected elder in 1840, hence was in office about 34 years.

Mr. John Cree was born in 1805, came to Chambersburg in 1826, and was ordained an elder Feb. 3, 1849. He was Superintendent of the Sabbath School for 16 years, and was ever active and zealous in the work of his Lord and Master, joining in the public prayer and in

JOHN CREE.

the social worship. In the spring of 1862 he moved to Pittsburg. On his return to this town a few years later, he felt it his duty to cast in his lot with the then feeble and struggling Central Church, and served as a member of its Session during the rest of his life. Feb. 21, 1890, he "came to his grave in a full age like as a shock of corn cometh in in his season." So long as he lived he did not cease to take a deep interest in the welfare of the Falling Spring Church and Sabbath School.

In the autumn of 1861, Messrs. Wm. G. Reed, Jas. C. Eyster, Frederick Byers, and Geo. F. Platt were chosen elders. Messrs. Eyster and Byers declined the honor, and the other two were ordained and installed on Dec. 7, 1861. In those troublous war times many changes took place in Church as well as in State, and the Session of the Falling Spring Church was not an exception to the general rule. As already said, Mr. Cree left in 1862. Soon after, I enlisted as a soldier. Not very long after my return from the army, the burning of the town occasioned the retirement of Mr. Holmes Crawford. A little later, the resignation of the Rev. S. J. Niccolls left the Church without a Pastor, and with only two ruling elders in charge. Although the Rev. J. B. H. Janeway accepted a call and was with us for several months, he was never installed nor did he join the Presbytery of Carlisle, so that the Church was without a Pastor until the installation of Dr. J. A. Crawford in July, 1867. I was young and inexperienced, had been reared in a Church of radically different polity, had never been a member of any other Presbyterian Church, and joined this one less than six months before my election to office. I therefore deferred to Mr. Reed in matters pertaining to the interests of the Church, and that prosperity and harmony prevailed to so great an extent throughout those years of unrest, is largely due, under God, to his wise and discreet management. Mr.

Reed was Superintendent of the Sabbath School six years, for a good many years was leader of the Church choir, and for more than half a century closely identified with the praises of the congregation in public and social worship.

On Feb. 1, 1869, Messrs. Frederick Byers, John H. Shumaker, and Jacob Sharpe Nixon were elected ruling elders. Mr. Byers again declined, and the others were installed on Feb. 21. The induction into office of these brethren gave the Church four office bearers either young or in middle life, who for more than fourteen years served together. During a considerable part of that time all were engaged in the Sabbath School, either as superintendent or as teachers. In 1872 the congregation, on the recommendation of the Session, adopted what was known as the Bellefonte or envelope system for its benevolent work, which resulted in doubling the contributions. After following that plan for three years, the congregation voted to return to the old system, which was followed by a decrease. At the end of the year 1876, the congregation voted unanimously to return to the envelopes, which have been used ever since, though not by all the members of the Church.

On May 15, 1883, a handsome sterling silver baptismal bowl was presented to the Church through the Session by Mrs. M. C. Washington.

DR. J. H. SHUMAKER.

In 1883, Dr. Shumaker was chosen Principal of the Academy at Blairstown, N. J., and left us in September of that year. The Session placed on record its great regret at parting with a brother beloved and honored in the Lord, and bore testimony to his great worth as a Christian and as an office bearer. In the fall of 1892, he returned to our town and was warmly welcomed by his many friends. After weary months of intense suffering, he was called up higher Feb. 7, 1894. Session placed on record a brief sketch of his life and labors and added the following: "We thank God that while he lived he helped to mould the characters of so many young men who have since attained to eminence in their various callings in life, and that thus his influence will be felt for good for many years to come. We honor the memory of our departed brother because of his personal character and record, and because of his fidelity to the varied and responsible duties which fell to his lot. We pay our tribute of affection to the sincere loving friend, the cheerful companion, the earnest consistent Christian. We extend our warm sympathy to the bereaved family, especially to her who for more than forty years has shared his inmost joys and sorrows, and pray that since her dearest earthly friend is removed, she may be able to trust wholly and entirely in that Friend who hath said, 'Lo, I am with you alway, even to the end of the world.' 'I am the Resurrection and the Life.'"

At a congregational meeting held March 15, 1885, the following were elected ruling elders: Henry A. Riddle, Wm. B. Reed, John S. McIlvaine, Robert E. Coyle, and John G. Orr. Mr. Coyle declined to serve and the others were installed on Sept. 12, of that year. All were at that time active in the Sabbath School and the prayer meetings, and have ever since discharged their official duties with a faithfulness and zeal worthy of the highest praise.

On Sept. 11, 1885, Mrs. Susan M. Crawford presented to

the Church through the Session a handsome pulpit Bible containing both the Authorized Version and the Revision of the New Testament.

On March 1, 1886, in response to the desire of a good many temperance advocates, and following the example of many other churches, a majority of the Session voted to cease the use of wine at communion, and to substitute therefor the unfermented juice of the grape.

On Jan. 1, 1891, Elder J. S. Nixon met with an accident which twelve days later terminated his earthly life. The following is a part of the minute adopted relating to him: "It is not the length of years we would emphasize, nor yet the number of positions he held, but the fact that all these years were filled with loving thoughts, with large service, and with efficient deeds; and that his official duties were discharged with such rare fidelity and earnest zeal as to prove a constant inspiration to all about him. Every department of Church work felt the impulse of his strong personality. He exerted a marked influence upon the lives of our young people by a sincere and genuine interest in them, to which also he ever gave happy expression; to those who were bearing the burden and heat of the day, his cheering and helpful presence gave

J. S. NIXON.

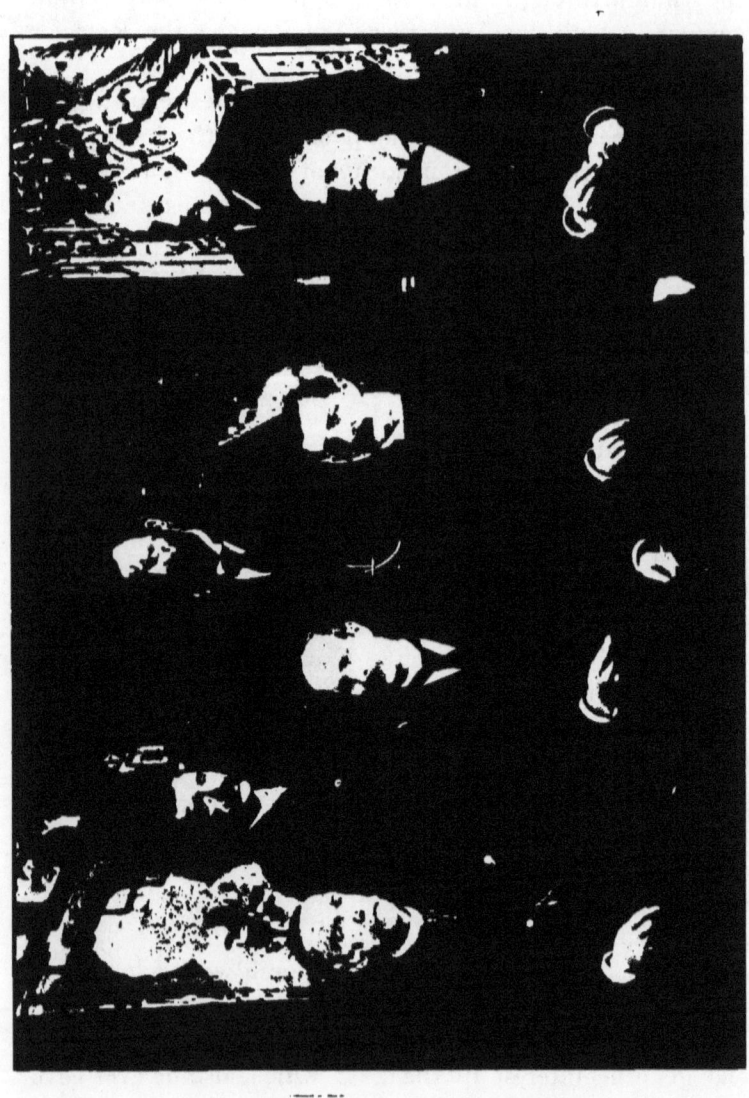

THE PRESENT SESSION.

J. S. McILVAINE. H. A. RIDDLE. G. F. PLATT. W. B. REED. H. K. SCHENCK. J. G. ORR. W. G. REED.

perpetual strength and encouragement, and to the aged, the sick, the afflicted, the outcast, he brought comfort in the hour of trial. A host of friends testify to his helpfulness, and now rise up to call him blessed."

Elder J. G. Orr took up his abode in Harrisburg in 1891, and now teaches a class in the Sabbath School of the Market Square Church, and is President of the Brotherhood of Andrew and Philip in that Church, but still retains his membership in this Session.

Throughout these years, covering the life of a generation, the members of Session have worked harmoniously together, and have been bound to one another by ties of close friendship and warm affection. In the last thirty-six years this congregation has had ten ruling elders. Two of them lived far beyond the period allotted to man; two went to their "long home" a good while before "the grasshopper" was likely to be "a burden;" the other six are still in service. Only two of the ten were children of the Falling Spring Church.

When Mr. Holmes Crawford resigned the clerkship, I was chosen his successor, much against my will, and have held the office ever since.

THE CHARTER.*

. AN ACT

For incorporating the Presbyterian Church of Falling Spring, in the County of Franklin.

WHEREAS sundry members of the Presbyterian Church of Falling Spring in the County of Franklin have, by their Petition, prayed that their Congregation may be incorporated, and by Law enabled, as a Body corporate and politic, to re-

---

*For the Deed, see page 39. The spelling and punctuation of the charter follow the original.

ceive and hold such charitable donations and bequests, as may from time to time be made to their society, and vested with such powers and privileges as are enjoyed by other religious Societies who are incorporated in this State.

AND WHEREAS it is just and right, and also agreeable to the true spirit of the Constitution, that the Prayer of the said petition be granted.

BE IT THEREFORE enacted, and it is hereby enacted by the representatives of the Freemen of the Commonwealth of Pennsylvania in General Assembly met, and by the authority of the same, That Patrick Vance, Esquire, Benjamin Chambers, Senior, Matthew Wilson, Esquire, Josiah Crawford, John Boggs, Esquire, Edward Crawford Junior, the Reverend, James Lang and James Moore, and their successors, duly elected and appointed in such manner as hereinafter is directed, be, and they are hereby made, constituted and declared to be a Corporation and body Politic in law and in fact, to have continuance forever, by the name, style, and title of "The Trustees of the Presbyterian Church of Falling Spring in the County of Franklin."

AND BE IT FURTHER ENACTED by the authority aforesaid, that the said Corporation and their successors, shall forever hereafter be persons able and capable in law, as well to take, receive and hold all and all manner of lands, tenements, rents, annuities, franchises and other hereditaments, which at any time heretofore have been granted, bargained, sold, enfeoffed, released, devised or otherwise conveyed to the aforesaid congregation of Falling Spring now under the pastoral care of the Reverend James Lang or to any other person or persons to their use, or intrust for them and the same lands, tenements, rents, annuities, franchises and other hereditaments are hereby vested and established in the said corporation and their successors, for ever, according to their original use and intention. And the said corporation and their successors are hereby declared to be seized and possessed with such estate and estates therein, as in and by the respective grants bargains, sales, enfeoffments, releases devises, or other conveyances thereof, is or are declared limited or expressed, as also that the said corporation and their successors, at all times hereafter shall be able and capable to purchase, have, hold receive and enjoy in fee simple, or of any other less estate or estates any lands tenements, rents, annuities, liberties, franchises and other hereditaments by the gift, bargain, sale alienation, enfeoffment, release, confirmation or devise of any person or persons, bodies politic or corporate capable and able to make the same, and further that the said corporation, and their successors, may take or receive any sum or sums of money, or any portion of goods or chattles that shall be given to them by any person or persons bodies politic or corporate, capable of making such gift or bequest, such money, goods and chattels, to be laid out and disposed of for the use and benefit of the aforesaid congregation, agreeably to the intention of the donors.

AND BE IT FURTHHR ENACTED by the authority aforesaid that the rents, profits, and interests, of the said real and personal estate of the aforesaid church and corporation, shall, by the said trustees, and their successors from time to time be applied and laid out for the maintenance and support of the gospel ministry in said congregation for repairing and maintaining their house of public worship, lots of land and other buildings, burial ground, and such pious and charitable uses, as shall be agreed on, and determined by a majority of the congregation at large called together on due notice to give their free vote in such case.

AND BE IT FURTHER ENACTED by the authority aforesaid, That when and as often as it may be necessary to rebuild enlarge or otherwise alter or repair the house of public worship, or any other buildings belonging to the aforesaid church and corporation, or to erect any new building, or to make any new purchases for the use of said congregation, then and in such case, it may be lawful for the aforesaid trustees and their successors, to make sale of or otherwise dispose of such part or parcel of the said estate real or personal, as a majority of the regular members of said congregation shall by their vote direct the money arising from such sale or disposal to be laid out and applied agreeably to the vote of the aforesaid majority.

AND BE IT FURTHER ENACTED by the authority aforesaid That the said trustees and their successors shall not by deed or any otherwise grant, alien, convey or otherwise dispose of any part or parcel of the estate real or personal in the said corporation vested, or to be hereafter vested, or change or incumber the same to any person or persons whatsoever, except in the manner and for the purposes herein before mentioned.

PROVIDED NEVERTHELESS, that no deed or other conveyance made by the said trustees or their successors bonafied and for valuable considerations for any part of the real estate of the said church and corporation in case the possession thereof pass immediately to the purchaser and continue in him his heirs or assigns, shall be called in question or invalidated for want of the consent of the majority of the regular members of the said church, unless the same be done within seven years from and after the sale and delivery of possession of such real estate to such purchaser or purchasers thereof.

AND BE IT FURTHER ENACTED by the authority aforesaid, That the said trustees or their successors, or a majority of them, may from time to time meet, as often as they may think necessary for the benefit of the said corporation, either on their own adjournments or on public notice from the pulpit, the preceding Lord's day immediately after divine service and before the congregation is dismissed or on regular notice in writing left at the house of each trustee; and the said trustees, being so met, be authorized and empowered, and they are hereby authorized and empowered to elect and appoint from among themselves a President; and also to elect and appoint from among themselves or other members of said congregation a Treasurer and Secretary, and to move, change, or continue all or either of them at pleasure, as shall seem to be most for the benefit of said corporation.

PROVIDED ALWAYS, that the meeting or meetings of said corporation be not called without the concurrence of two or more trustees or of three or more respectable members of said congregation with the president, or without the particular business there to be done, and reasons of the meeting being specified in the notification.

AND BE IT FURTHER ENACTED by the authority aforesaid the said trustees or a majority of them, met, as is herein directed before shall be authorized and empowered, and they are hereby authorized and empowered, to make rules by laws and ordinances, and to do everything needful for the government and support of the secular affairs of said congregation.

PROVIDED ALWAYS, that the said by laws and ordinances or any of them be not repugnant to the laws of this Commonwealth and that all their laws and proceedings be fairly and regularly entered into a book to be kept for that purpose.

AND BE IT FURTHER ENACTED by the authority aforesaid, That the said corporation and their successors shall have full power and authority to make have and use one common seal with such device and inscription as they shall think proper, and the same to break alter and renew at their pleasure.

AND BE IT FURTHER ENACTED by the authority aforesaid That the said corporation and their successors by the name of the trustees of the Presbyterian Congregation of Falling Spring in the County of Franklin shall be able and capable in law to sue and be sued plead and be impleaded in any court, or before any judge or justice in all and all manner of suits, complaints, pleas, causes, matters and demands of whatever kind, nature or form they may be; and all and every matter or thing therein to do in as full and effectual a manner as any other person or persons bodies politic or corporate within this Commonwealth may or can do.

AND BE IT FURTHER ENACTED by the authority aforesaid, That the said corporation shall always consist of eight members called and known by the name of the Trustees of the Presbyterian Congregation of Falling Spring, and the said members shall at all times hereafter be chosen by ballot, by a majority of such members, met together of the said congregation as shall have been enrolled, as stated worshippers with, and yearly contributors to the support of the said congregation, for at least the space of one year.

PROVDED ALWAYS, that the pastor or minister of said congregation for the time being shall be entitled to vote equally with any member of said congregation; and also, that all and every person or persons qualified to vote and elect as aforesaid, shall and may be also capable of being voted and elected a trustee as aforesaid, provided he or they be not more than two years in arrear for pew rent, due the said church and congregation.

AND BE IT FURTHER ENACTED by the authority aforesaid, That the said Patrick Vance Esquire, Benjamin Chambers Senior, Matthew Wilson Esquire, Josiah Crawford, John Boggs Esquire, Edward Crawford Junior, the Reverend James Lang and James Moore, the first and present trustees hereby incorporated shall be and continue trustees until removed in manner following viz: one fourth part in the number of said trustees, being the fourth part herein first named, shall cease and discontinue and their appointment determined on the first Monday of April, which will be in the year of our Lord seventeen hundred and eighty-six; and the second fourth part herein mentioned, shall cease and discontinue and their appointment determine on the first Monday in April which will be in the year one thousand seven hundred and eighty-seven and in like manner the appointment of the third fourth part herein mentioned shall cease and determine on the first Monday in April which shall be in the year seventeen hundred and eighty-eight, and the appointment of the last fourth part shall cease and determine on the first Monday in April which shall be the year one thousand seven hundred and eighty-nine; on which days in each of the aforementioned years respectively new election shall be held of other trustees, instead of those whose appointments shall have ceased and determined; which manner of discontinuance determination, new appointments or election shall be continued on the first Monday of April in every year hereafter forever, so that no person shall be or continue a trustee longer than four years together without being reelected; which may be done whenever and as often as the members of said congregation qualified to vote, as aforesaid described, shall think fit.

PROVIDED ALWAYS, That whenever any vacancy shall happen by the death refusal to serve, or other removal of any one or more of the said trustees, or in case the members of the said church shall neglect to meet on the first Monday of April, in any year, an election shall be held, as soon as conveniently can be done, and some fit person or persons chosen and appointed as before directed, to supply such vacancy; and that the remaining trustees have power to call a meeting of the electors of said congregation for that purpose.

PROVIDED ALWAYS, and it is hereby enacted by the authority aforesaid, That the clear yearly value interest or income of the lands, tenements, rents, annuities or other hereditaments and real estate of the said corporation shall not exceed the sum of three hundred and fifty pounds of gold or silver money, at the current value thereof in the Commonwealth of Pennsylvania, exclusive of pew rents and other free contributions belonging to the aforesaid congregation, which said money shall be received by the said trustees and disposed of by them, for the purposes and in the manner hereinafter described and directed.

Signed by order of the House
JOHN BAYARD Speaker.

Enacted into a law at Philadelphia on Friday the twenty-fifth day of March in the year of our Lord, one thousand seven hundred and eighty-five.

SAM'L. BRYAN
Clerk of the General Assembly.

Enrolled 21st July A. D. 1785.

THE HISTORY OF THE TRUSTEES,

BY JOHN M. M'DOWELL, ESQ.

To the writer has been assigned the duty of speaking on behalf of the Trustees of the Falling Spring Presbyterian Church, and of writing the history or an account of the different buildings and property of said Church. From the somewhat meagre data attainable by the writer he offers the following:

Col. Benjamin Chambers, the founder of Chambersburg, about the year 1730, settled on or near the Falling Spring, or between that stream and the Conococheague near their junction. Others soon followed him, forming what he

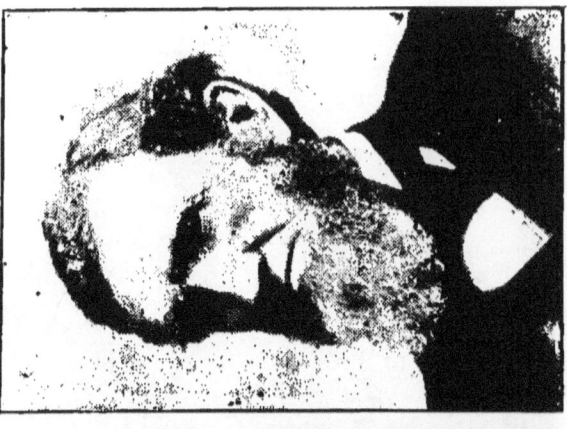

CAPT. BENJAMIN CHAMBERS,
Son of the Founder of Chambersburg, Pa.
Born in 1755. Died Dec. 29, 1813.

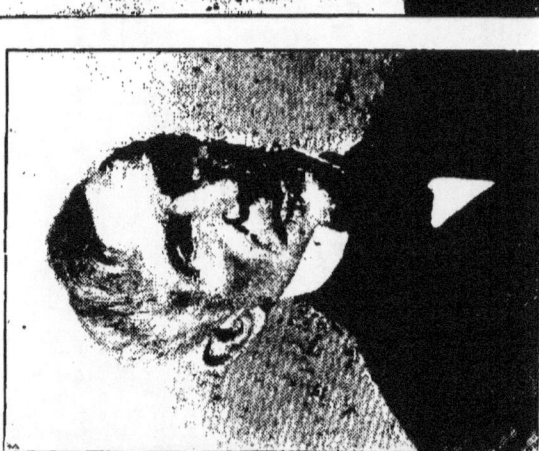

JUDGE GEORGE CHAMBERS.
Son of Capt. Chambers. Born Feb. 24, 1786.
Trustee for about fifty years prior to Nov. 16,
1861. Died Mch. 25, 1866.

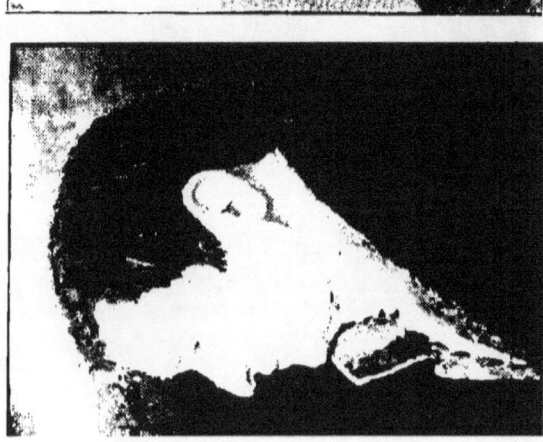

WM. L. CHAMBERS,
Son of Judge Chambers. Born Jan. 13, 1823.
Trustee, 1861-1876, 1881-1889. Died Apr. 26, 1889.

called "The Falling Spring Settlement." Col. Chambers and most, if not all the pioneer settlers in this valley, were Presbyterians or Blue Stockings. Among the first buildings erected by our forefathers, after putting up log cabins to shelter them from the heat, cold and rain, were small log buildings for school houses and places for worship. The church and the schoolhouse went together, generally, at first one house being used for both purposes. Col. Chambers early gave the romantic cedar grove on the bank of the Conococheague Creek for a graveyard, schoolhouse and church. In this grove, near the spot where the present church stands, was erected at a very early date, certainly before 1739, and very probably about 1737, a small log building which was used as a schoolhouse and place of worship. It was built of rough logs, with doors on the east and southern sides, and lighted by two long narrow windows, of the width of two small panes of glass, "running the entire length of the northern and western sides of the building." This building was small and exceedingly plain. When this building, or "study-house," as it was called, would not hold or accommodate the congregation, it is said that in mild weather, they would resort to the saw-mill of Col. Chambers, which he had erected on what was called the "Island," near the junction of the Creek and Falling Spring, just across the latter from the present woolen mill and south of the residence of James E. Elder. On the green sward surrounding the saw-mill, the congregation would sit or stand, and listen to the minister preaching from the saw-mill as a pulpit and shelter. It is thought that prior to the building of the "study-house" or first log church, preaching was had at this saw-mill, as the congregation was organized and had supplies sent them from Donegal Presbytery before 1737.

In 1767, this old rough log building gave place to a

larger and more pretentious edifice built of hewed logs, which was about thirty-five feet wide, and seventy feet long. It stood upon the same spot as the present church occupies, the front of the building facing east. The following agreement was made and executed by the Trustees of the congregation to the builder of the Church:*

"We, in the name of the Falling Spring Congregation, do promise to pay or cause to be paid to James Shanks or his assigns, the sum of forty-five pounds of the currency of Pennsylvania, for the building of a meeting house at the Falling Spring, and when said house is built and sufficiently done, the money is to be paid, as witness our hands and his, 5th day of July, 1767.

"Benjamin Chambers, John Dixon, Richard X Venable, Matthew Wilson, Wm. Gass, Patrick Vance, Benjamin Gass, Robt. Jack, Thomas Burney."

Test,
George Latmer,
Archibald Brown.

This better church cost then in our money about $220.00. But little though it seems, the Trustees would not pay for it until "sufficiently done." No advance payment when under roof or during the progress of the building, as is generally provided for now in building contracts, but no money was to be paid until the "house is built and sufficiently done."

On January 1, 1768, Col. Chambers donated the cedar grove and tract of land on which the church was built, to the congregation, and he and his wife Jean executed a deed therefor, which is recorded in the Recorder's office of Franklin County, in Deed Book Vol. A, pages 210, 211 and 212. (See this History, p. 39.) The consideration mentioned in

---

*For this agreement and much other information, I am indebted to an article published in 1851 in the *Valley Sentinel*, and written by the late Dr. William C. Lane. The original agreement was burned in the fire of 1864.

the deed was the yearly rental of "one Rose if required." The purposes and uses to which the land so granted and donated were to be put, were as follows: for "a Meeting House or Presbyterian Church, Session House, School House, or any other Seminary of Learning, (Dancing Schools, play Houses and all such sinful exercises excepted,) Burying Place or Graveyard, and such Religious Purposes as said congregation may think proper and find necessary for the publick Worship of God."

In 1803 the log church was removed because, I presume, the congregation wanted a better and more modern one. In its place and on its site a substantial stone church building was erected. This was a plain, simple, unpretentious, but neat and beautiful edifice, being the same building we now

occupy, though not so long. As the minutes of the Board of Trustees prior to 1864 and other records were destroyed in the great fire of that year, we are unable to give the cost of this building, or any of the transactions of the congregation or Board of Trustees until 1864.

About 1840 a two story brick Lecture and Sunday School

building was erected on the southeast corner of the church property, extending over on land belonging to the Hon. George Chambers and given by him to the congregation so long as this building should be used for religious purposes.

On August 25, 1842, the Hon. George Chambers donated to the congregation, as an addition to the cemetery, a lot on the southern side of that portion of the grant by Col. Benj. Chambers used as a burial ground, and a lot on the northern side of said burying ground. This deed is recorded in Deed Book, Vol. 33, page 104.

' In 1857, during the Rev. Joseph Clark's pastorate, the church building of 1803 was enlarged and altered, as seen

in the picture. A large door was put in the centre of the front wall, where the window now is, leading into a vestibule, from which entrance was made into the audience-room through two doors at either side, and from which stairs led up to the gallery over the vestibule, where the choir sat until 1866, when it was brought down to the back part of the church. The congregation gradually increased in numbers and more pews were wanted. In August, 1868, it was determined to make the following alterations and improvements: The cupola was taken off, the gallery removed, the vestibule thrown into the church, two doors made, one in each tower, a large window put in, in place of the front door, stained glass windows put in, a platform or raised floor placed in front of the large window for the choir, and the ceiling removed and the present one put on; and in 1869 a new and handsome walnut pulpit was placed in the church by Col. and Mrs. Thos. B. Kennedy at their expense, and a pulpit table presented by Mr. Leonard B. Kindline. No record is made of the cost of these improvements, although a subscription was taken up therefor.

After the revival of 1876 the old Lecture Room on the corner seemed inadequate to accommodate the increased attendance at the weekly meetings of the congregation. On October 18, 1876, a Building Committee was appointed to invite and receive bids for a "new Lecture-room and Sabbath-School Building." After a number of joint meetings of the Trustees and the congregation to consider the question of a new building,

THE DENNY MEMORIAL.

the present chapel was decided upon, and erected in 1877-8 at a cost of $5899.89.*

The old Lecture-Room was torn down, sold and removed, and part of the land on which it stood reverted to the heirs of its donor.

In the fall of 1883 a new furnace was put in the church at a cost of $341.52.†

In 1885 a pipe organ was purchased from Hook & Hastings, of Boston, by a committee (appointed by the Organ Association, which had been in existence some time raising funds for this purpose,) and placed in the annex which was built in the rear of the church by the Trustees, the church was painted inside and out, new glass placed in the windows, a new slate-roof put on, the church wainscoated, pews lowered, &c., at a total cost of $5468.18, the cost of the organ being $2400.00, the repairs and annex the balance.

THE THOMSON MEMORIAL.

Frank Thomson, Esq., of Philadelphia, in 1889 made a donation to the church of $100.00, which was by the Trustees set apart as a nucleus for a manse fund. This was added to by legacies from

---
*For pictures of the Church and Chapel as they are to-day, see frontispiece.
†Two memorial windows have been placed in the Church, the Denny Memorial in 1887, and the Thomson Memorial in 1892.

Miss Margaret Denny, Mrs. Martha L. Woods and Mrs. Emily Lane, making the fund in all in 1892 about $2500.00, which the Trustees had set apart as a manse fund. At a congregational meeting in February, 1892, the question of the congregation securing a house for its pastor was raised and discussed, and a committee appointed to confer wtth the Trustees on the subject. After several conferences and the raising of about $2500.00 by the committee by subscription, the present manse and former residence of Mrs. Alice McGowan was purchased for $6200, and the deed for the same given the congregation, November 4, 1892.

In addition to the aforementioned property of this church, sufficient money was raised by voluntary subscription in 1890, principally by the exertions of our former pastor, the Rev. Jno. G. Hibben, and his estimable wife, to purchase from Dr. Robt. C. Hays a lot of ground on West Loudon Street, 60 feet wide by 60 feet deep, and erect thereon a neat and substantial frame building about 35 by 50 feet, for a Chapel or Mission Sunday-School, at a total cost, (including a furnace put in this fall, largely the donation of Prof. M. R. Alexander and Mrs. T. B. Kennedy,) of $771.59. A deed for this lot was duly executed to the Church.

On March 25, 1785, an Act of the Legislature was passed chartering this congregation by the corporate name of "The Trustees of the Presbyterian Church of Falling Spring in the County of Franklin."* Since that date its property and temporal affairs have been managed by a board of eight Trustees. The Act of Incorporation provides for eight Trustees to be elected on the first Monday of April annually by the contributors to the Church and the Pastor, two to be elected each year to serve four years. This Act is recorded in Law Book No. 11, page 474.

---

*For this Charter see page 129.

The revenue of the Church for payment of Pastor's salary, light and fuel, sexton, and other expenses, has, I think, been derived from the rentals of the pews ever since the second log church was erected. These rentals have been payable quarterly, except during the year 1876, when they were paid weekly by envelopes. Since January 1, 1877, they have been payable quarterly. In 1866 the rentals from pews amounted to $1970.00. In 1868 they were increased, amounting to $2550.00, if all the pews were rented. In 1876 all the pews were assessed an additional ten per cent, and in 1882 they were increased twenty per cent more. The revenue from pew rents has rarely been sufficient to meet the annual expenses, leaving a deficit every few years, to be made up by voluntary subscriptions from the congregation. All buildings, improvements and repairs have generally been paid by subscriptions. The church proper is now free from debt, and has been thus free for several years.* Except the last year or two, the church has generally had a debt, large or small, resting on it. When Dr. J. A. Crawford was called in 1867, he was given a salary of $1300.00 and house rent. In 1868, his salary was increased to $1800.00 per annum, and has continued at that figure ever since. In 1887 Dr. Crawford was made *Pastor Emeritus* at a salary of $300.00.

All the records having been burned, I have no means of ascertaining the names and time of service of the Trustees from 1768 to 1864, except from the memory of the older members of our church, and as few of our present members can name the present Trustees, so our older members can give me but few names of those serving the church prior to 1864. I have appended hereto a list of all the names of Trustees that I have been able to collect. From the building agreement of 1767 I get the names of the nine Trustees signing that

*There is still a mortgage on the Manse of $2300.00.

Born in Franklin Co., Pa., Jan. 12, 1789. Elected a Ruling Elder in 1840. Superintendent of the Sabbath School for some years prior to 1846. Died Aug. 2, 1848.

paper. In the deed of Benjamin Chambers of January 1, 1768, one year later, are given the names of the then Trustees, and I presume that Benjamin Chambers was also a Trustee at that time. . The Charter gives the names also of the first eight Trustees who served from date of charter until their successors were elected.

Prior to 1864, the only persons that we know certainly served this church as Trustees from the date of its charter in 1785, were Col. Benjamin Chambers, who served until 1787, when "on account of his advanced age and infirmities he asked leave to resign." The seven others are mentioned in the charter. Mr. Joseph Chambers was an active, zealous, and efficient member of the Board until his death in 1851. He was the father of Mrs. Lucy C. George of our Church. The Hon. George Chambers resigned November 14, 1864, having, as he said in his letter of resignation, been a Trustee for about fifty years, and a very useful, faithful, and efficient member he was. Dr. Samuel D. Culbertson, J. Smith Grier and John Cree were trustees in 1857, but how long before that year I know not.

Since 1864 there have been but twenty-two Trustees. It seems to have been the rule in this church, that once a person was elected a trustee, he continued to be such until promoted to a higher stewardship in the world beyond. Our honored President, Col. Thos. B. Kennedy, has been a Trustee since 1857, and President of our Board since the resignation of Judge Chambers in November, 1864. Mr. Samuel M. Linn has faithfully served our church since 1865, our efficient Secretary, Benjamin Chambers, Esq., has been a member of our Board continuously since 1876, and three of us since 1883, the Hon. John Stewart since 1889, and J. W. Sharpe, Esq., since 1891. Unless the precedent established is disregarded, we may all look forward to dying in the service, and having it said of us, if nothing else, "he was a Trustee of Falling Spring Presbyterian Church for ten, twenty, or fifty years," as the case may be. More interest should be taken by our church members in the election and annual meeting of the Congregation. I have attended nearly every annual meeting for the past twenty years, and do not think I have seen twenty persons present at any one meeting. This should not be. At the annual meeting held last April (1894), a resolution was adopted, asking the Trustees to call the next and subsequent annual meetings in the evening, instead of early morning as heretofore. This will be done, and we trust a better attendance will thus be secured, and the interest and prosperity of this dear old church advanced, and many precious souls be here saved and enrolled among its members.

In addition to the Trustees in service in 1767, as named on page 138, and in 1768, and those named in the charter, as found on page 130, all we know of the Trustees prior to 1864 is as follows:

Col. Benjamin Chambers was re-elected in 1786. Whether others also were, we have no means of ascertaining.

The Hon. George Chambers served from 1814 until 1864, when he resigned. Joseph Chambers served to the date of his death in 1851. Dr. Samuel D. Culbertson, John Cree, and J. Smith Grier were Trustees in 1857, how much earlier is not known.

The following is a list of the Trustees since 1857: Col. Thomas B. Kennedy, 1857– ; W. H. McDowell, 1861–65; James C. Eyster, 1861–70; Wm. L. Chambers, 1861–76, 1881–89; Wm. G. Reed, 1861–83; Dr. Edmond D. Culbertson, 1861–76, 1882–83; Samuel M. Linn, 1865– ; Dr. George F. Platt, 1865–66, 1870–74; Wm. McLellan, 1865–81; James C. Austin, 1866–68; J. S. Nixon, 1868–91; John P. Culbertson, 1874–82; Benjamin Chambers, 1876– *; Robert

---

*Benjamin Chambers, Esq., died April 4, 1895, after the above paper was read

E. Coyle, 1876-81; Daniel O. Gehr, 1881-83; Wm. B. Reed, 1883- ; John L. Grier, 1883- ; John M. McDowell, 1883- ; Hon. John Stewart, 1889- ; Joshua W. Sharpe, 1891- .

The following have served as Presidents of the Board, as far as known: Hon. George Chambers, for many years prior to his resignation in 1864; Col. Thomas B. Kennedy, 1864- .

The following have served as Secretaries of the Board: Wm. L. Chambers, 1864-76; Benjamin Chambers, 1876- .

The following have served as Treasurers of the Church: W. H. McDowell, 1864-65; J. S. Nixon, 1865-66; Wm. G. Reed, 1866-Jan. 3, 1876, when he resigned; J. S. McIlvaine, 1876-Jan. 13, 1877, when he resigned; Wm. G. Reed, 1877- .

BENJAMIN CHAMBERS.

The following have served as Sextons of the Church: John Schofield, for some time prior to 1864; Allen Smith, 1864 to Feb. 10, 1868, when he resigned; Josiah E. Schofield, 1868-1877; Peter Helfrick, 1877- .

SKETCH OF THE SABBATH SCHOOLS,

BY J. S. M'ILVAINE.

In the year 1816—or thirty-five years after Robert Raikes founded the first Sunday-School in England,—the godly women of Chambersburg seeing many of the youth of the town growing up in ignorance and in utter disregard of the Lord's Day, resolved to organize a Sunday-School for their spiritual and mental improvement; and a meeting for the purpose of considering the question was called, of which Rev. David Denny was the Chairman. It was resolved, that a school be immediately started; and Miss Elizabeth Riddle and Miss Catharine Crawford were appointed to act jointly as Superintendents.

The school at first was for girls only, and was called the "Female Sunday-School," and was held in the Academy. Soon after, a school for boys was started in another room of the same building by Mr. Blood, Mr. Ross, Mr. Winters and a few other gentlemen. Finding the boys hard to manage without the persuasive influence of the ferule and birch, which were so potent in the control of the week-day schools of that period, their zeal flagged and the school was disbanded. Some of the boys, however, were persuaded to attend the girls' school. The school was undenominational, and teachers and scholars represented all churches of the town.

After some years denominational schools were organized, and the original school, which from the first was composed largely of the members of the Falling Spring Church and congregation, became the school of that Church. Both white and colored children were admitted to the school, and this practice was continued until the organization of the Colored Mission School. The colored children at first were mostly slaves, and in one class taught by Mrs. Cree there were three slaves owned by the Hon. George Chambers.

From this, together with the fact that free schools had not yet been organized, we may reasonably conclude that the instruction given was largely of a secular character, not, however, to the exclusion of wholesome religious truths and the elementary doctrines of religion. Miss Elizabeth Ross succeeded the Misses Riddle and Crawford as Superintendent.

About 1820 the school was transferred to the Grand Jury room on the second floor of the Court House, and Miss Rebecca Riddle became Superintendent. After her marriage to the Rev. Dr. Schneck in 1829 she resigned. The school was then removed to the Presbyterian Church, and Mr. McCracken became Superintendent; he was succeeded by Mr. Albert Beatty, who served but a short time, when he left town. The Hon. Judge Thomson succeeded him, and held the office until 1846, and was followed by Mr. John Cree. Mr. Cree entered the school as a teacher in 1829, just before its removal from the Court House to the Presbyterian Church. He continued in office as Superintendent sixteen years, resigning in 1862. He was succeeded by Mr. William G. Reed, who has been a Ruling Elder since 1861, and who is one of the few remaining links uniting the past with the present. Mr. Reed continued in charge of the school until March 1868. He was succeeded by Elder George F. Platt, who continues to this day the Superintendent of the school, and to whose faithful and efficient services of over a quarter of a century is largely due its present prosperous condition. Durin the first eighteen years of Dr. Platt's superintendency he was absent from the school but six times; for eight and one-half years he was at his post at the opening of the school without a single exception;—a record of faithful and conscientious performance of duty probably not surpassed by any superintendent of a Sabbath-School in the land.

Previous to 1868 there was no infant department in the

school. In the spring of that year an infant class was organized under the care of Mrs. Eliza Aston, but for some reason was for a time disbanded. Some time after, it was reorganized, and, under the management of Miss Fannie Reed, flourished, and has continued ever since to be one of the most interesting and hopeful departments of the Church. Miss Reed resigned on her marriage to Rev. Frank Newton, and has been serving the Lord faithfully in the Mission work in India since 1870. This department has since been in charge, successively, of Mrs. Rose Senseny, Miss Emma Smith, Miss Maggie Chambers, Miss Emily B. Lane, Mrs. Rebecca Pomeroy, Mrs. Martha Orr, Miss Sallie Reed, and is now under the care of our Pastor's wife, Mrs. Schenck, with Miss Madge Nelson as her assistant.

There is connected with the school a colored Mission school which originated as follows: In the early part of the war a large number of colored people, taking advantage of the opportunity of escaping from slavery, fled north, and many of them stopped here. Rev. Henry Reeves, who then had charge of the Rosedale Seminary, moved with pity for them in their wretched poverty and ignorance, conceived the idea of gathering them, with the other colored people of the town, into a Sabbath-School. He first organized the school in his academy, and his lady teachers soon became deeply interested in the scholars, as they made such rapid progress and were so hungry for knowledge.

About the year 1863 Mr. Reeves removed to Philadelphia, and in 1864 Mr. William G. Reed, who had been one of his assistants, took charge of the Mission and it was transferred to the Chapel of the Falling Spring Church, and continued there until the Chapel was torn down. For some time after, the school met in the basement of the Baptist Church at the foot of Queen Street. One of the great features of this school was the singing; many of the refugees having fine voices, and the melody of 200 voices or more poured forth with the heart, if not with the understanding, in the beautiful hymns of Moody & Sankey, aroused them to the highest pitch of entusiasm and drew crowds of appreciative listeners.

This Mission school died out for some years, but was revived, or rather a new organization was formed during the ministry of Rev. John Grier Hibben, who, with his estimable wife, took a deep interest in the wretched condition of the people living in what is know as Wolfstown, and were instrumental in building what is known as the "Wolfstown Mission Chapel" of the Falling Spring Church, and in starting the school which has continued since 1890, to pour fourth its healing balm upon the festering wounds which sin has made, bringing joy to many sad and sorrowing hearts.

This school has been for the last three years under the efficient Superintendency of Mr. John M. McDowell. The present school is composed of 52 scholars in the senior department, 21 in the primary class, with 12 teachers, and 2 officers.

The following are the officers and teachers of our Church school to-day: Dr. George F. Platt, Superintendent; John S. McIlvaine, Ass't. Sup't.; Frank M. Duncan, Sec'y. and Librarian; Thos. H. Wallace, Assistant; Mrs. Nellie B. Hoopes, Organist; Mrs. H. R. Schenck, Principal of the Primary Department. Teachers: Mrs. James F. Kennedy, Mrs. M. C. Washington, Mrs. T. M. Nelson, Mrs. J. W. Sharpe, Mrs. Alice Grier, Mrs. H. W. Spessard, Miss Emma Smith, Miss Nana Stewart, Miss Mary Craig, Miss Scott King, and Messrs. W. B. Reed, H. A. Riddle, J. M. McDowell, A. Nevin Pomeroy, J. W. Sharpe, William Lusk, J. S. McIlvaine and Samuel T. Clifton.

In this brief and rapid sketch of the Falling Spring Sabbath-School, we cannot stop to dwell upon the work of the many faithful teachers who have served in this most delightful and profitable field of the Church, and have gone up to their rest and to their reward; we may, however, without invidious distinction name a few of those who were first in the field and did pioneer work. In connection with Miss Riddle and Miss Crawford, the first superintendents of the original Sunday-School, should be named—Miss Margaret Plummer, Miss Rebecca Riddle, Miss Mary McDowell, Miss Mary Peach, Miss Elizabeth Ross and Miss Susan Chambers, all of whom gave of their time, hearty sympathy and prayers to the cause. Some years later, among the saintly women who served the Lord in this field was Mrs. Frances Culbertson, wife of Joseph Culbertson, Esq., familiarly known as "Aunt Frances." She was one of the most faithful, earnest and self-sacrificing women of her time. She was "instant in season and out of season;" her heart over-flowed with sympathy for the poor and the outcast; she was *the* friend of the colored people of the town, and was a teacher in their Mission school for many years. She was filled with a consuming zeal for the spread of the gospel in heathen lands, organizing the first Female Missionary Society in Carlisle Presbytery, and gave her two sons to the ministry, one of whom, the Rev. Simpson Culbertson, was a missionary in China for eighteen years; his dust reposes in the midst of the people to whom he gave the translated Bible, and the best part of his life.

But we must not trespass further upon your time and patience, for it were vain for mortal pen to attempt to write the history of all these seventy-eight years; only God knows, and Eternity alone can reveal the result of these long years of labor in this most fruitful garden of the Lord.

HISTORY OF THE MISSIONARY SOCIETIES.
BY MRS. WM. B. REED.

In this, the one hundredth anniversary of our beloved

church, we have reached a point where it is well for us to look back over the way we have come, and review what has been done in obedience to the command of Christ, "Go ye therefore, and teach all nations, baptizing them in the name of the Father, and of the Son, and of the Holy Ghost."

It was during the pastorate of the Rev. David Denny, that the first band of workers in response to the call of the Misses Margaretta and S. A. Chambers, met in the parlors of Mrs. Geo. Chambers, Sr., and on that summer afternoon about the year 1834, the first Foreign Missionary Society of the Falling Spring Church was organized, with Miss Rebecca Riddle, afterward Mrs. Schneck, as President; Miss Anna Chambers, Secretary; and Miss Alice Denny, Treasurer. I quote the words of one who was present at that meeting, Mrs. Jane Senseny, then Miss Jane Davis: "A more faithful and earnest band of workers could not be found, the savor of whose lives still lingers in the daughters, granddaughters, and nieces in the Church to-day."

During the pastorate of the Rev. Daniel McKinley early in the forties, Home Mission work was begun. Boxes were packed and sent to gladden the hearts of the noble workers at the outposts, and as the true spirit of Home Missions is to "begin at Jerusalem" and work outwards, the ladies of the Church, under the leadership of Mrs. Frances Culbertson, did all they could, by visiting and praying with the poor and depraved of town, to bring to them a knowledge of Christ and His love.

Owing to the stormy times during the war, the work languished. But the "Macedonian cry" was growing louder and louder, and the "Come over and help us" could not be neglected any longer. In the year 1871, with the aid of Dr. Crawford, who was then Pastor of the Church, the present Woman's Foreign Missionary Society was organized, with Mrs. Eliza Aston, President; Miss Margaretta Chambers, Treasurer; and Mrs. J. S. Nixon, Secretary, an office she held, and the duties of which she most faithfully performed for more than twenty years until her death, when she heard the Master's "Well done." The dues were fixed at one dollar a year, and eight collectors were appointed; of that number Miss Lizzie Gilmore and Mrs. Alice Grier are still serving.

But it was not until 1876 that regular meetings were held. At that time there was a change of officers, and it was decided to hold regular meetings opened with devotional exercises. These have been continued either monthly or bi-monthly until the present time. In 1878, the Presbyterial Society was organized. Our Society then became auxiliary to that, and since that time there has been a steady growth. The members now number 63, and the amount raised has yearly increased from an average of $85.00 the first few years, to $234.00 in 1894. The officers have been since organization: Presidents, Mrs. Aston, Mrs. Robt. E. Coyle, Mrs. T. B. Kennedy, and Mrs. Jas. F. Kennedy; Vice-Presidents, Mrs. McIlvaine, Mrs. M. R. Alexander; Secretaries, Mrs. J. S. Nixon, and Mrs. Alice Grier; Treasurers, Miss Margaretta Chambers, Miss Lizzie McDowell, Miss Emma Smith, and Miss Mary Bard.

Of the Home Mission work there is no record of a formal organization until 1885, but soon after the war the work of preparing boxes for missionaries was again taken up, and every year with few exceptions, one and sometimes two boxes were sent, the value of these boxes ranged from $150.00 to $300.00. In 1885, the present Woman's Home Missionary Society was organized as auxiliary to the Presbyterial Society, with Mrs. Ellen McLellan, President; Mrs. Rose Senseny, Vice-President; Mrs. J. S. McIlvaine, Recording Secretary; Mrs. Jas. F. Kennedy, Corresponding Secretary; and Mrs. J. G. Orr, Treasurer. It was decided, however, that the old line of work should be continued, and that the annual dues should go toward the preparing of the boxes, all other money raised to go through the Presbyterial Society. This has been done with the exception of one year, when no box was sent, and the money was given toward the building of a chapel in Wolfstown, a part of the town where Gospel work was very much needed. Regular monthly or bi-monthly meetings have been held, and the interest in this work is each year increasing. The Society now numbers sixty members, and the amount raised the past year was, cash, $107.01, value of box, $200.00, total, $307.01. The only change in officers until 1894, has been that of Treasurer, Mrs. Chauncey Ives now holding that office. In 1894, Mrs. McLellan resigned, and Mrs. Rose Senseny was elected President, Mrs. Harry Riddle, Vice-President, the other officers remaining the same.

On the afternoon of Feb. 21, 1881, Dr. Crawford called a meeting of the young ladies of the Church, and twenty-nine responded. He tried to impress upon them the need of the Church for young workers, and their duty to the Church, and especially to the work of Foreign Missions, so dear to his own heart. The seed then sown was watered by an address by Miss Loring, given at the annual Presbyterial Meeting held at Greencastle, and attended by one of our young ladies, Miss Anna Linn, who on her return called a meeting at her home, which resulted, March 31, 1881, in the organization of the Young Ladies' Branch for Foreign Missions, with 25 members.* The following officers were elected: Mrs. W. B. Reed, President; Mrs. Dan Kennedy, Vice-President; Miss Maggie Chambers, Secretary; and Miss Anna Linn, Treasurer. Besides the giving of annual dues, the members have taken orders for work of any kind that they could do, to raise money for the cause, and their faith

---

*This list of members will be found on pages 108 and 109.

has been strengthened and their zeal increased by seeing their work prosper. They now have a membership of forty-nine, and a yearly increase in the amount raised from $88.00 the first year to $253.00 in 1894. A very pleasant feature has been the annual Thankoffering, which was started by them in 1885, and since followed by the other societies with great success. It is largely due to the encouraging words and deeds of Dr. Crawford, who started them on the way with the motto: "Let us not be weary in well doing: for in due season we shall reap, if we faint not," that they have held from the first the position of the Banner Branch of the Presbytery. The officers since organization have been: President, Mrs. W. B. Reed; Vice-Presidents, Mrs. Dan Kennedy, Mrs. M. R. Alexander, Mrs. Wm. Nixon, and Mrs. Nevin Pomeroy; Secretaries, Miss Maggie Chambers, Mrs. Theo. Shumaker, Miss Grace McLanahan, Miss Nettie King, Miss Nana Stewart, and Miss Mary Platt; Treasurers, Miss Anna Linn, Miss Annie McDowell, and Miss Alice McKnight.

In 1883, Mrs. Wm. McLellan started a band among the little girls, called the "Busy Bees." This was in the interest of Foreign Missions. They worked so well that for a number of years they were the Banner Band of the Presbytery. In 1887, Mrs. McLellan was obliged to give it up, and for about a year nothing was done. It was then taken by Mrs. Hibben and Miss Sallie Reed, and was changed from a Foreign to a Home Band. A scholarship was then taken at $75.00 a year, and this pledge has been faithfully met each year. They have also done a great deal at Christmas, in sending boxes away, the one sent last year being valued at $20.00, and also doing work at the same time for for the Mission school at Wolfstown, thus bringing Christmas cheer to those who otherwise would have little. The band is now under the direction of Mrs. Joshua W. Sharpe and Mrs. Schenck, Bessie McKnight being the Secretary, and Elizabeth Riddle the Treasurer.

In 1887, a band composed of boys and girls was organized by Mrs. John G. Orr, and called the "Band of Trust," to work for the Home Mission cause, but at the close of the year, when the band of "Busy Bees" was changed to a Home Mission band, as many of the girls were members of that, it was thought best to re-organize, and they then became the "Boys' Home Mission Band." They now have fourteen members, and the amount raised the past year was $33.44. They have met with many discouragements, but have persevered, and have done much for the Master. I am very glad to record this Boys' Band, and may they grow up to manhood as workers for the Lord. Miss Mary Clarke and Miss Scott King now have charge of the Band. .

Our Church has also been represented in foreign lands by the Rev. Simpson Culbertson in China, who has been called to his reward and has heard the Master's "Well done, good and faithful servant: enter thou into the joy of thy Lord;" and also by Miss Fannie Reed, who left as Mrs. Frank Newton in 1870 for India, where she now labors with her husband and daughters. May there be others who will hear the call and answer, "Master, here am I; send me, send me."

Thus we see that, for more than fifty years, work has been done in obedience to our Master's parting command. But each step in advance makes another imperative, and the ever-widening opportunities bring added responsibilities. May we so improve them, that, at the last, it may be said of the Falling Spring Church as of the Church of Philadelphia, "I know thy works: behold, I have set before thee an open door, and no man can shut it: for thou hast a little strength, and hast kept my word, and hast not denied my name."

HISTORY OF THE YOUNG PEOPLE'S SOCIETY OF CHRISTIAN ENDEAVOR,

BY WM. B. REED.

For the past few days we have been dealing with the early history of this Church, and the further back we could go, and call up an honored and glorious past, the better. It cannot be so with my theme to-night. For the Young People's Society of Christian Endeavor cannot boast of its great age, but as the youngest child of the Church must, notwithstanding its youth, ask a place side by side with any of the subjects before considered.

Many of the ways of Church work of to-day would seem very strange indeed to those whose lives and deeds we are now celebrating. But an advance in Christian work is only in keeping with a like advance all along the line of the activities of the age in every direction. As in the natural world, the world of business, the methods employed now could not have been even dreamed of or predicted fifty years ago, so the methods of Christian work to-day must at least keep step with the same advance in other directions. Along this line is the Young People's Society of Christian Endeavor. It is but 13 years since Dr. Clark, the Pastor of a Congregational Church in Portland, Maine, feeling the needs of a more active work among the young people of his Church, called a meeting for the purpose of considering the subject, and from that meeting resulted the formation of the first Y. P. S. C. E. So well adapted was it to the wants of the young, and so heartily did they fall in with the work, that from the first the growth in numbers, power and influence was such that the little spark became a flame, and spread until the torch thus lighted shone from town to town in New England, from state to state, from land to land, until to-day it is acknowledged to be one of the evangelizing forces of modern times, yes, the most wonderful world-wide Christian movement of the age. Who will say God's smile does not rest upon it? Verily it is no work of man's, or long since would it have come to naught; "but if it be of God, ye cannot overthrow it."

Our Session very often in its meetings spoke of the necessity of a like Society in our Church, and at its meeting on January 9, 1888, after earnest discussion of the subject appointed a committee, consisting of our Pastor Mr. Hibben, John G. Orr and William B. Reed, to look into the matter and take such action as they might deem best. This Committee conferred with a number of the active workers in the Church and reported favorably to the Session, Feb. 6, and as a result we have the organization of our Young People's Society in March of 1888, the first Society in our city, if not in the county. Our first officers were: Mr. T. M. Nelson, President; Mrs. Wm. G. Nixon, Secretary. The "Ironclad Pledge" was adopted, and the Society was launched with great interest. From the first, we found the work pleasant and well suited to our young people, and they have ever responded nobly to any calls for Christian work asked of them.

We met at first on Friday evenings for prayer, but this was afterwards changed to Sabbath evenings before Church services, at which time we still meet. We started with about 25 members, and now have on our roll 51 active and 7 associate members. The work was not without opposition at first, but now we feel that our people generally are heartily in sympathy with it. Our average attendance now is perhaps 50 to 60 every Sabbath evening. The meetings are interesting, and the pledge is, I think, faithfully kept. The work does not consist of merely a meeting for prayer, but the several committees, Lookout, Prayer-meeting, Executive, Social, Floral, Music, and Good Literature Committees give plenty of work for all our members. And while all these committees have been very faithful, I think the Floral Committee deserves great credit for its work. These beautiful flowers we see on the pulpit, and these decorations we have from time to time, are their work, and tell of their faithfulness. Special commendation must be given to the committee now in charge, whose Chairman, Miss Bessie McKnight, has never failed since her appointment, to give some flowers each Sabbath, if they were at all to be had. These flowers, after serving their purpose in the Church, are sent with messages of love and sympathy to the sick, and many a sick room has thus been cheered by the ministrations of this committee. The Social Committee has also given us some pleasant entertainments. Among these may be mentioned three very interesting lectures, one by the Rev. David H. Riddle on "Lord Macaulay," one by the Rev. John K. Demorest, D. D., on "Mary Queen of Scots," and one by one of our worthy Presidents, Joshua W. Sharpe, Esq., on "Egypt."

The work, while not what we should like to have it, yet we trust is such that we are making some progress. Of our present membership, at least 22 have been won from associate membership, and have united with the Church, and are now enrolled as active members. And thus are we developing and keeping up an interest in Church work among the young. Our present list of officers is as follows: President, John G. Wiestling; Vice-President, Miss Arie Kennedy; Second Vice-President, Miss Mary Craig; Corresponding Secretary, Miss Bessie McGowan; Recording Secretary, Frank M. Duncan.

We are glad to be a part of the mighty host whose numbers have reached the grand total, according to the report at the Cleveland Convention last July of 33,700 Societies, with a membership of 2,023,800, from whose ranks, says the same report, last year 183,650 associate members have united with the Church and are now active workers in this glorious cause. By the same report we are told that $225,000 found their way into the treasuries of the different Church Boards, for Home and Foreign Missions, from the Y. P. S. C. E. The work moves on. Who can estimate the power for good of this consecrated host, the very flower of the Church, as they take their places and exert their influence for good in every direction in the Church and in the world? Our prayer is that the work may not lag, but go forward and upward until we shall all be called home to exchange the Cross for the Crown, and when we shall have sung for the last time on earth our Christian Endeavor Parting Song, "God be with you till we meet again."

OFFICERS.

NOV. 12, 1894.

Pastor.

Harris R. Schenck, 225 North Main Street.

Elders.

Dr. George F. Platt, 1861, William B. Reed, 1885,
William G. Reed, 1861, John S. McIlvaine, 1885,
H. A. Riddle, 1885, John G. Orr, 1885.

Clerk of Session—Dr. George F. Platt.

Trustees.

Term Expires 1895.

William B. Reed, Joshua W. Sharpe, Esq.

Term Expires 1896.

Hon. John Stewart, Benj. Chambers, Esq., Sec'y.*

*After Mr. Chambers' death, Mr. T. M. Nelson was elected to fill the vacancy and Mr. J. M. McDowell was elected Secretary.

Term Expires 1897.
Thomas B. Kennedy, Prest.   Samuel M. Linn.
Term Expires 1898.
John L. Grier,   John M. McDowell, Esq.

Treasurer.
William G. Reed, 447 East Market Street.

Musical Director.
H. A. Riddle.

Organist.
Miss Anna W. Stewart.

Superintendent of Church Sabbath School.
Dr. George F. Platt.

Superintendent of Mission Sabbath School.
John M. McDowell.

Superintendent of Industrial School.
Mrs. T. B. Kennedy.

President of Woman's Foreign Missionary Society.
Mrs. James F. Kennedy.

President of Woman's Home Missionary Society.
Mrs. Rose Senseny.

President of Young Ladies' Branch for Foreign Missions.
Mrs. William B. Reed.

President of Girls' "Busy Bees" Mission Band.
Mrs. Joshua W. Sharpe.

Superintendents of Boys' Home Mission Band.
Miss Mary Clarke and Miss Scott King.

President of Young People's Society of Christian Endeavor.
John G. Wiestling.

Superintendent of Little Light Bearers.
Miss Bessie S. McGowan.

Sexton.
Peter Helfrick, 80 West King Street.

FORM OF RECEPTION OF MEMBERS.

NOTE.—It is to be remembered that the admission of members is committed to the Session of the Church. Besides this PRIVATE admission it is our custom to call upon new members to make the following *public* avowal of their faith in Christ and their engagement to be the Lord's. Of course those absent from these occasions, by voluntarily remaining in our membership, renew this covenant as solemnly and as truly as if present, and are bound by their holy vows of obedience and helpfulness and attendance.

This pledge which we take unto God is solemn in its nature and serious in its consequences.

BELOVED IN THE LORD:

The Session having already received and enrolled you as *a member* of this Church, you are now to be publicly recognized by giving your assent to the substance of Christian faith as follows:

The Church of God is not of man's appointment. The great Head of the Church and Creator of all men formed believers into the Household of Faith.[a] Our Lord bade His disciples "confess" Him "before men," and the Holy Ghost, speaking through the apostle Paul, declares that "if thou shalt *confess with thy mouth* the Lord Jesus, and shalt believe in thine heart that God hath raised Him from the dead, thou shalt be saved."[b]

Being moved, as we trust, by the Holy Ghost, to join *yourself* to the people of God, you have now come to make public acknowlegement of this your desire and purpose.

We believe in one living and true God, Father, Son and Holy Ghost, Creator and Ruler of all, infinitely perfect and worthy of love, worship and obedience.[c]

We believe in one Saviour, Jesus the Christ, God manifest in the flesh, who in His life fulfilled the Law, and by His death atoned for our sins and makes us worthy, by His grace, of fellowship with Him.[d]

---

a Eph. 1:10, 22, 23; Col. 1:18; Eph. 5:23, 27, 32.
b Mt. 10:32, 33; Rom. 10:9-10.
c Deut. 6:4; 1 Cor. 8:4-6; Mt. 28:19; 2 Cor. 13:14.
d John 1:1, 14; 1 Tim. 3:16; Mt. 5:17; 1 Peter 1:19, 20; 1 Tim. 2:6; 1 Cor. 1:30.

We believe in one Holy Spirit, who convinces of sin, renews the heart, and transforms the life.ᵉ

We believe in one Rule of doctrine and duty, the Holy Scriptures, the divinely inspired and infallible guide.ᶠ

We believe in one condition of salvation, faith in the Lord Jesus Christ, manifest in godly sorrow for sin, and in a godly life.ᵍ

We believe in one Church of God, embracing all who are united to Christ by saving faith and divine grace.ʰ

We believe that the holy Sacraments of the Christian Church are Baptism and the Lord's Supper; the *former* signifying and sealing our union with Christ, the forgiveness of our sins, and our engagement to be the Lord's;ᵏ and the *latter* by giving and receiving bread and wine according to Christ's appointment,ˡ showing forth His death and the communion of His people with Him by faith, and giving spiritual nourishment and growth in grace to those who worthily receive it.

We believe that the Christian Sabbath is to be kept holy to the Lord by abstinence from all works except those of necessity and mercy, and by proper attendance upon divine worship as due to God alone.ᵐ

We believe in the Resurrection of the dead.ⁿ

We believe in a coming judgment for all mankind, when men will be judged according to the deeds done in the body, and when the wicked shall go away into eternal punishment, and the righteous into eternal life.°

Confessing this as your faith, you are now to enter into formal covenant with God and this Church.

---

e John 16:7-14; 2 Thess. 2:13.
f 2 Tim. 3:15-17; 2 Peter 1:19; 1 Thess. 2:13.
g Eph. 2:8; Rom. 1:16-32; 2 Cor. 7:10; Is. 55:7.
h Eph. 1:10, 22, 23; 1 Cor. 12:12-13.
k Mt. 28:19; 1 Cor. 11:23-26; Rom. 4:11; Col. 2:1'-12; Gal. 3:27; Acts 2:38.
l 1 Cor. 11:23-29; 1 Cor. 10: 16, 17, 21.
m Gen. 2:3; Ex. 20:8-11; Is. 56:2, 4-7; Is. 58:13-14; Mt. 28:1; John 20:1, 19, 26; Acts 20:7; 1 Cor. 16:1-2; Rev 1:10; Mt. 5:17-18; Neh. 13:15-21.
n 1 Cor. 15:42-44; John 5:28-29.
o 1 Cor. 4:1-5; 3:13-15; 2 Cor. 5:9-10; Rom. 14:10-12; Acts 10:42; Mt. 25:14-46; Rev. 20:12-15.

[ADDRESS TO THOSE BAPTIZED IN INFANCY.]

You, having been baptized in infancy, are now to come into *full communion* with the Church whose external privileges you have already enjoyed. By your voluntary choice of Christ, and by your saving faith in Him, you are now, we trust, no longer, *an heir* merely of covenant privileges, but of salvation also. The vows and obligations assumed in your behalf by Christian parents in your baptism, you do now ratify and confirm. With your own hand you subscribe unto the Lord, set your seal to the covenant with God, and declare "I am the Lord's." You hereby deliberately separate *yourself* from all that is worldly, from all that may hinder your own close fellowship with Christ, or that may bring reproach upon his Church.ᵖ

Do you thus promise?

[ADDRESS TO THOSE NOT HITHERTO BAPTIZED.]

You, who have not hitherto enjoyed even outward membership in the Church of God, now, in the presence of God, His holy angels, and this assembly, formally separate *yourself* from the world,ᵖ that you may take your place as a "*fellow-citizen* with the saints, and the household of God." Let your baptism this day be in reality the "putting away of the filth of the flesh," and the "putting on" of the Lord Jesus Christ.

[Here let baptism be administered.]

And now, beloved, renouncing the world, the flesh, and the devil, you do solemnly covenant that you take God the Father to be your God, the Lord Jesus Christ to be your Saviour and Master, and the Holy Spirit to be your Sanctifier.

You take the Word of God as your Rule of faith and practice.

You take the people of God to be your people.

---
p 2 Cor. 6:14-18; 7:1; 1 John 2:15-17; Rom. 12:2; 14:21; 1 Cor 8:9-12.

You do now give *yourself* up, soul and body, time and talents, powers and possessions, your business and your pleasures, all that you have, are, or shall be, unto Jesus Christ, to be His and serve Him forever, and at His sovereign disposal in all things.

You promise, *in reliance on Divine grace*, to continue in communion with God's people, by a regular attendance on the Word and ordinances, by a walk and conversation as becometh the Gospel, and by submitting to the discipline of the Church as here administered.

To this covenant do you give your cordial and hearty, consent, promising by God's help to keep your consecration unto the end?

[ADDRESS TO THOSE RECEIVED BY LETTER.]

Having already publicly confessed Christ, you to-day renew your covenant with God and transfer your relations to this Church. May God give you grace to renounce the world, to honor God, and to promote the spread of the Gospel, the peace and good name of the Church, and the salvation of souls.

To this end do you therefore, in the presence of God, give your hearty and cordial assent to the covenant of this Church, as just read?

[ADDRESS TO ALL THE NEW MEMBERS.]

Do you, relying only upon God's grace, promise to be faithful to the interests of this Church; to labor with it in all works of Christian well-doing; to attend upon *all* its ordinances *so far as you may be able*;[q] to submit to its discipline;[r] and in all things to study its peace, its prosperity, its usefulness, its good name, and its upbuilding on the most holy faith?

Do you promise to its Pastor, its Elders, and to its mem-

---
[q] Heb. 10:24-25.
[r] 1 Thess. 5:12-13; Heb. 13:17; 2 Thess. 3:6, 10-15; Titus 1:10-13; Mt. 18:15-18.

bers severally the offices of kindly affection with brotherly love; of sympathy, hospitality and charity; and that you will in all things study to promote their welfare in spiritual things, to the end that we may mutually grow in grace and in the knowledge of our Lord and Saviour Jesus Christ?

[Here let the church-members rise.]

In the name of the Lord Jesus Christ, we the officers and members of this Church, do now affectionately welcome you to our membership and fellowship in this Household of Faith.

And we, on our part, while solemnly renewing hereby our own covenant, engage to walk with you in all lowliness of mind, and to watch over you as *an heir* with us of a common grace and hope.

We promise to you our brotherly sympathy, counsel and help, so long as you shall continue with us as *a member* of the body of Christ.

We humbly pray for Divine help, that God would enable us, by His Grace, to fulfill the solemn covenant which we have taken on our souls, and that we may be faithful to each other, and together seek the present and eternal welfare of our fellow disciples, and "do good unto all men, especially unto them who are of the Household of Faith."

And now, beloved, I charge you every one before God and the Lord Jesus Christ, who shall judge the quick and the dead at His appearing and His Kingdom, that you walk worthy of your high vocation, adorning the doctrine of God your Saviour in all things; living henceforth no longer unto yourselves, but unto Him who loved you and gave Himself for you. And now unto Him who is able to keep you from falling and to present you faultless before the presence of His glory with exceeding joy, to the only wise God our Saviour, be glory and majesty, dominion and power, both now and ever. Amen.

[While standing, let the Church sing, "Blest be the tie that binds."]

ROLL OF COMMUNICANTS.

The list given herewith embraces only the names of those persons more or less actively identified with the Church on Nov. 12, 1894. A number of names appear on the records of Session which are names of persons either unknown to the Session or who have passed beyond the jurisdiction of the Session, or who have been retired from active membership for reasons indicated in the extracts from the Constitution of the Presbyterian Church.

The year indicates the date of admission to the Church. "P" and "C" indicate respectively that such persons were admitted on profession or by certificate. "T" indicates that the person whose name it follows was a teacher either in the home school or in the Wolfstown Mission, on Nov. 12, 1894.

A supplementary list is added, repeating, according to years of reception, the names of those who were on our roll before the time of Dr. Niccolls, the senior ex-Pastor, and who are still on the roll.

The following extracts from the Constitution are printed for the information of the Church.

I. Who are the Church.

Form of Government, Chapter II, Sections 1, 2, 3, 4: "Jesus Christ, who is now exalted far above all principality and power, hath erected, in this world, a kingdom, which is His Church." (Eph. 1:20–23; Ps. 2:6.) "The Universal Church consists of all those persons in every nation, together with their children, who make profession of the holy religion of Christ, and of submission to His laws." (Rev. 5:9; Acts 2:39; 1 Cor. 1:2 compared with 2 Cor. 9:13.) "As this immense multitude cannot meet together in one place, to hold communion, or to worship God, it is reasonable, and warranted by Scripture example, that they should be divided into many particular churches." (Gal. 1:21, 22; Rev. 1:4, 20; Rev. 2:1, &c.) "A particular church consists of a number of professing Christians, with their offspring, voluntarily associated together, for divine worship and godly living, agreeably to the Holy Scriptures; and submitting to a certain form of government." (Acts 2:41, 47; 1 Cor. 7:14; Acts 2:39; Mark 10:14, compared with Matthew 19:13, 14, and Luke 18:15, 16; Heb. 8:5; Gal. 6:16; 1 Tim. 5:17; Rom. 12:7, 8; Acts 15:25; Matt. 18:15–20; 1 Cor. 5:4, 5; Heb. 13:17; 1 Thess. 5:12, 13, and 1 Tim. 5:17; 2 Thess. 3:6, 14, 15; 1 Cor. 11:27 to the end. (As to the relations of the children of professing Christians, see under the Roll of Baptized Members.)

II. The Reception of Members, and other Duties of the Session.

Form of Gov. IX, 6: "The Church Session is charged with maintaining the spiritual government of the congregation; for which purpose, they have power to inquire into the knowledge and Christian conduct of the members of the Church; to call before them offenders and witnesses, being members of their own congregation, and to introduce other witnesses, where it may be necessary to bring the process to issue, and when they can be procured to attend; to receive members into the Church; to admonish, to rebuke, to suspend, or exclude from the sacraments, those who are found to deserve censure; to concert the best measures for promoting the spiritual interests of the congregation; and to appoint delegates to the higher judicatories of the Church." (Heb. 13:17; 1 Thess. 5:12, 13 and 1 Tim. 5:17; Ezek. 34:4; 2 Thess. 3:6, 14, 15; 1 Cor. 11:27 to the end; Acts 15:2, 6.)

Directory for Worship, x, 3, 4: "Those who are to be admitted to sealing ordinances, shall be examined as to their knowledge and piety." "When unbaptized persons apply for admission into the Church, they shall, in ordinary cases, after giving satisfaction with respect to their knowledge and piety, make a public profession of their faith, in the presence of the congregation; and thereupon be baptized."

Digest, 803: "Universalists are not to be admitted to sealing ordinances."

Digest, 805: "It is the province of the Session to judge of the qualifications of candidates for membership in the Church."

Digest, 807: "In no ordinary circumstances can a person give good evidence of a readiness to obey Christ in all things, who, having the opportunity, does not connect himself with some particular branch of the visible body of Christ."

III. Jurisdiction over Members.

Book of Discipline, IV, 18: "original jurisdiction, in relation to members, pertains to the Session."

Bk. of Disc., XI, 108: "The judicatory, to which a Church member belongs, shall have sole jurisdiction for the trial of offences whenever or wherever committed by him."

109: "A member of a Church, receiving a certificate of dismission to another Church, shall continue to be a member of the Church giving him the certificate, and subject to the jurisdiction of its Session (but shall not deliberate or vote in a Church meeting, nor exercise the functions of any office), until he has become a member of the Church to which he is recommended, or some other evangelical Church; and, should he return the certificate, within a year from its date, the Session shall make record of the fact, but he shall not thereby be restored to the exercise of the functions of any office previously held by him in that Church."

XII, 114: "When any member shall remove from one Church to another, he shall produce a certificate, ordinarily not more than one year old, of his church-membership and dismission, before he shall be admitted as a regular member of that Church.

"The names of the baptized children of a parent seeking dismission to another Church shall, if such children are members of his household and remove with him and are not themselves communicants, be included in the certificate of dismission. The certificate shall be addressed to a particular Church, and the fact of the reception of the person or persons named in it shall be promptly communicated to the Church which gave it."

116: "If a Church member, more than two years absent from the place of his ordinary residence and Church connections, applies for a certificate of membership, his absence, and the knowledge of the Church respecting his demeanor for that time, shall be distinctly stated in the certificate."

VII, 48: "If a communicant, not chargeable with immoral conduct, inform the Session that he is fully persuaded that he has no right to come to the Lord's Table, the Session shall confer with him on the subject, and may, should he continue of the same mind, and his attendance on the other means of grace be regular, excuse him from attendance on the Lord's Supper; and, after fully satisfying themselves that his judgment is not the result of mistaken views, shall erase his name from the roll of communicants, and make record of their action in the case."

49: "If a communicant, not chargeable with immoral conduct, removes out of the bounds of his Church, without asking for or receiving a regular certificate of dismission to another Church, and his residence is known, the Session may, within two years, advise him to apply for such certificate; and, if he fails so to do, without giving sufficient reason, his name may be placed on the roll of suspended members, until he shall satisfy the Session of the propriety of his restoration. But, if the Session has no knowledge of him for the space of three years, it may erase his name from the roll of communicants, making record of its action and the reasons thereof. In either case, the member shall continue subject to the jurisdiction of the Session. A separate roll of all such names shall be kept, stating the relations of each to the Church."

50: "If any communicant, not chargeable with immoral conduct, neglects the ordinances of the Church for one year, and in circumstances such as the Session shall regard to be a serious injury to the cause of religion, he may, after affectionate visitation by the Session, and admonition if need be, be suspended from the communion of the Church until he gives satisfactory evidence of the sincerity of his repentance, but he shall not be excommunicated without due process of discipline."

52: "If a communicant renounces the communion of this Church by joining another denomination, without a regular dismission, although such conduct is disorderly, the Session shall take no other action in the case than to record the fact, and order his name to be erased from the roll. If charges are pending against him, these charges may be prosecuted."

[NOTE—Owing to the fact that difficulties of various kinds have confronted the Session in compiling this list, it is not unlikely that errors may be found in it, notwithstanding the great care taken. The Session will be grateful for any corrections.]

Alexander, Mrs. Margaret H., (1883,) C.
Alexander, Milton R., (1883,) C.
Andrews, Miss Mary E., (1893,) P.
Andrews, Mrs. Sarah, (1860,) C.
Aughinbaugh, Miss Carrie, (1893,) P.
Aughinbaugh, Miss Mary C., (1884,) C.
Bard, Miss Louisa J., (1861,) P., T.
Bard, Miss M. Blanche, (1893,) P.
Bard, Miss Mary P., (1859,) P.
Beatty, Mrs. Margaret T., (1848,) P.
Bickley, Mrs. Catharine, (1890,) C.
Bitner, Miss Carrie N., (1894,) P.

Bitner, Mathias, (1894,) P.
Blair, Andrew, (1882,) C.
Blair, A. Sloane, (1893,) P.
Blair, Mrs. Mary S., (1882,) C.
Bowman, Mrs. Annie R., (1875,) C.
Bowman, Benjamin, (1876,) P.
Bowman, Miss Elizabeth C., (1893,) P.
Bowman, Miss Harriet R., (1893,) P.
Boyd, Mrs. Catharine, (1879,) C.
Boyd, Miss Grace G., (1893,) P.
Boyd, Miss Helen R., (1893,) P.
Brendle, Miss Elva E., (1892,) P.
Brewer, Mrs. Isabella W., (1877,) C.
Byers, Miss Anna, (1861,) P.
Caufman, Mrs. Jeanette M., (1866,) C.
Chambers, Mrs. Abigail McE., (1850,) P.
Chambers, Benjamin, (1876,) P.*
Chambers, George, (1883,) C.
Chambers, George, Jr., (1889,) P.
Chambers, Miss Eleanor, (1887,) P.
Chambers, Mrs. Ellen, (1854,) P.
Chambers, Mrs. Emeline K., (1846,) P.
Chambers, Miss Laura B., (1876,) P.
Chambers, Miss Margaret, (1866,) P.
Chambers, Miss Mary E., (1866,) P.
Clark, Mrs. Anna M., (1853,) C.
Clark, David C., (1869,) C.
Clark, Miss Eva S., (1893,) P.
Clark, James C., (1894,) P.
Clark, Mrs. Margaret E., (1869,) C.
Clark, Miss Roberta S., (1889,) P.
Clarke, John C., (1890,) C.
Clarke, Mrs. Kate M., (1890,) C.
Clarke, Miss Katharine B., (1893,) P.
Clarke, Miss Mary E., (1890,) C.
Clarke, Miss Susan, (1892,) P.
Clendenin, Milton A., (1880,) C.

*Died Apr. 4, 1895.

Clippinger, Mrs. M. L., (1894,) C.
Cooper, Miss Clare T., (1892,) P.
Coyle, Mrs. Blanche B., (1869,) C.
Coyle, Robert E., (1876,) P.
Craig, Miss Carrie, (1882,) C.
Craig, Miss Mary, (1882,) C., T.
Craig, Thomas C., (1878,) P.
Crandall, Miss Elsie C., (1890,) P.
Crawford, Miss Ellen A., (1879,) P.
Crawford, Mrs. Susan M., (1867,) C.
Criswell, Andrew M., (1845,) P.
Criswell, Miss Henrietta A., (1889,) P.
Criswell, Miss Nancy R., (1887,) P.
Criswell, Robert T., (1887,) P.
Culbertson, Mrs. Ellen K., (1843,) P.
Culbertson, Mrs. Julia, (1870,) C.
Curriden, George A., (1893,) P.
Curriden, Mrs. Kate, (1871,) C.
Curriden, Miss Margaret Grace, (1890,) P., T.
Daniels, Mrs. Agnes C., (1870,) P.
Douglas, Miss Louisa, (1852,) C.
Downey, Mrs. Agnes, (1893,) C.
Duncan, Frank M., (1893,) P., Lib.
Duncan, Mrs. Mary M., (1861,) P.
Edgar, Mrs. Elizabeth, (1884,) C.
Edgar, John B., (1894,) P.
Edmondson, Mrs. Bertha B., (1885,) C.
Elder, Mrs. Margaretta, (1889,) P.
Elder, Mrs. Mary E., (1873,) P.
Elliott, Mrs. Mary H., (1886,) C.
Elliott, Samuel B., (1884,) P.
Eyster, Mrs. Margaret, (1889,) P.
Fields, Mrs. Eliza S., (1890,) P.
Fields, Miss Elmira M., (1890,) P.
Finney, Miss Eleanor May, (1890,) P.
Finney, Miss Florence G., (1890,) P.
Gardiner, Mrs. Alice S., (1866,) P., T.

PRESBYTERIAN CHURCH.   175

Gehr, Mrs. Isabel R., (1893,) C.
George, Mrs. Lucy C., (1858,) P.
George, Miss Sallie M., (1893,) P.
Gillespie, Mrs. Annie, (1890,) P.
Gillespie, Harry S., (1890,) P.
Gilmore, Mrs. Harriet B., (1861,) P.
Gilmore, Miss Lizzie G., (1861,) P.
Gilmore, Walter B., (1892,) P.
Gordon, Cyrus H., (1892,) P.
Gordon, Mrs. Mary L., (1866,) P.*
Greenewalt, Harry C., (1876,) P.
Greenewalt, Miss Jane R., (1890,) P.
Greenewalt, John C., (1890,) P.
Greenewalt, Miss Margaret B., (1893,) P.
Greenewalt, Mrs. Martha, (1872,) P.
Greenewalt, Mrs. Mary D., (1890,) C.
Greenewalt, Miss Nancy C., (1890,) P.
Grier, John L., (1854,) P.
Grier, Miss Mary F., (1857,) P.
Hall, Mrs. Jennie C., (1877,) P.
Hambright, Mrs. Frances B., (1886,) C.
Hambright, George W., (1886,) C.
Hambright, Miss Letitia J., (1881,) P.
Hambright, Miss Sarah J., (1893,) P.
Hayman, Miss Kate W., (1858,) P.
Helfrick, Mrs. Maria E., (1872,) P.
Helfrick, Peter, (1872,) P.
Hibben, Mrs. Jenney D., (1888,) C.
Hoke, Clarence J., (1893,) P.
Hoke, Miss Harriet Ethel, (1893,) P.
Hoke, Harry E., (1890,) C., T.
Hoke, Mrs. Mary B., (1890,) C.
Hoke, Mrs. Sarah R., (1881,) P.
Holmes, Wesley B., (1892,) P.
Hoofman, Mrs. Elizabeth, (1870,) P.
Hoopes, Mrs. Nellie McI. (1891,) C.
Housum, Mrs. Lucy S., (1855,) C.

*Died, Nov. 26, 1894.

Huber, Mrs. Elizabeth, (1852,) C.
Ives, Miss Charlotte B., (1892,) P.
Ives, Miss Ellen C., (1889,) P.
Ives, Mrs. Emma C., (1866,) P.
Jacoby, Miss Ella Belle, (1890,) P.
Jacoby, Mrs. Susanna, (1893,) C.
Johnson, Mrs. Annie C., (1891,) P.
Jones, George, (1893,) P.
Jones, Miss Grace H., (1891,) P.
Jones, Mrs. Mary D., (1893,) P.
Jones, Thomas B., (1894,) P.
Karper, Mrs. Clara G., (1876,) P.
Kennedy, Mrs. Ariana R., (1852,) P.
Kennedy, Miss Ariana, (1886,) P.
Kennedy, Mrs. Cora H., (1890,) C.
Kennedy, Miss Helen L., (1893,) P., T.
Kennedy, James S., (1890,) P.
Kennedy, Mrs. Louisa W., (1859,) C., T.
Kennedy, Mrs. Margaret C., (1892,) C.
Kennedy, Mrs. Mary, (1890,) C.
Kennedy, Thomas B., (1854,) P.
Kindline, Leonard B., (1866,) P.
King, Miss Annetta, (1883,) P.
King, Edward C., (1881,) P.
King, Miss Elizabeth McC., (1876,) P.
King, Miss Margaretta S., (1871,) C.
King, Mrs. Mary, (1848,) P.
King, Miss Mary S., (1886,) P.
King, Miss M. Scott, (1883,) P., T.
King, Miss R. Christina, (1874,) P.
Langdon, Miss A. Jessie, (1888,) P.
Langdon, Averett L., (1884,) P.
Langdon, Mrs. Georgiana, (1883,) P.
Lesher, Benjamin B., (1893,) P.
Lesher, Mrs. Tillie N., (1882,) C.
Leslie, Miss Edith, (1880,) P.

Leslie, Miss Ellen, (1872,) P.
Leslie, Miss Florence C., (1876,) P.
Leslie, Mrs. Matilda K., (1868,) C.
Lindsay, Mrs. Catharine, (1849,) C.
Linn, Mrs. Jane, (1863,) C.
Linn, Samuel C., (1863,) C.
Little, Miss Nancy J. F., (1886,) C.
Ludwig, Mrs. Emma B., (1891,) P.
Lusk, William, (1893,) C., T.
MacAllen, William S., (1892,) C.
Maclay, David, (1879,) P.
Maclay, Miss Lydia E., (1868,) P.
Maclay, Mrs. Mary P., (1879,) C.
McDowell, Miss Annie C., (1876,) P.
McDowell, Mrs. Clara C., (1880,) C.
McDowell, Mrs. Eliza G., (1866,) P.
McDowell, John M., (1875,) P., T., Supt.
McDowell, Miss Lizzie M., (1866,) C.
McDowell, Mrs. Martha, (1863,) C.
McDowell, Miss Minnie A., (1866,) P.
McDowell, Wilken Brewer, (1880,) P.
McDowell, William H., (1856,) C.
McFadden, Thomas S. R., Jr., (1894,) P.
McGowan, Mrs. Alice C., (1866,) P.*
McGowan, Miss Annie T., (1893,) P.
McGowan, Miss Bessie S., (1893,) P.
McIlvaine, John S., (1875,) C., T.
McIlvaine, John S., Jr., (1887,) P.
McIlvaine, Mrs. Mary, (1875,) C.
McKibben, Miss Mary, (1871,) C.
McKnight, Miss Alice S., (1886,) P.
McKnight, Miss Elizabeth A., (1892,) P.
McLanahan, Miss Grace G., (1876,) P.
McLellan, Mrs. Ellen, (1850,) C.
Martin, Charles C., (1892,) P.
Martin, Mrs. Emma, (1892,) P.

---

*Died, Dec. 9, 1894.

Mehaffey, Mrs. Ellie C., (1877,) P.
Mehaffey, Mrs. Mary, (1873,) C.
Mellinger, Mrs. Margaret E., (1884,) P.
Myers, Miss Cora, (1890,) P.
Nelson, A. Howard, (1889,) P.
Nelson, Mrs. Annie H., (1873,) C., T.
Nelson, Miss Margaret McD., (1889,) P., T.
Nelson, Miss Sallie J., (1892,) P.
Nelson, Thomas M., (1873,) C.
Nelson, Tom McD., (1893,) P.
Orr, John G., (1883,) C.
Orr, Mrs. Martha H., (1883,) C.
Platt, Clarence N., (1887,) P.
Platt, George F., (1861,) C., Supt.
Platt, Mrs. Mary N., (1864,) C.
Platt, Miss Mary N., (1890,) P., T.
Pomeroy, A. Nevin, (1874,) C., T.
Pomeroy Mrs. Belle McL., (1880,) P.
Pond, Miss Jennie C., (1890,) C.
Ramsay, Mrs. Carrie M., (1892,) C.
Ramsay, Robert W. (1893,) P.
Reed, Mrs. Elizabeth S., (1891,) C.
Reed, Mrs. Eliza H., (1871,) C.
Reed, Frederick B., (1891,) P.
Reed, John H., (1871,) C.
Reed, J. Ross, (1889,) P.
Reed, Mrs. Rebecca L., (1843,) P.
Reed, Mrs. Sadie E., (1881,) P.
Reed, William B., (1866,) P., T.
Reed, William G., (1843,) P.
Ritchey, Mrs. Ella R., (1885,) C.
Riddle, David H., (1893,) P., T.
Riddle, Miss Elizabeth B., (1891,) P., T.
Riddle, Henry A., (1882,) C., T.
Riddle, Mrs. Martha H., (1882,) C.
Rosenberry, Miss Elmira M., (1887,) P.
Ross, Mrs. Annie V., (1876,) C.
Rote, Miss Josephine, (1861,) P.
Rowe, Mrs. Annie E., (1888,) C.

Ryerson, Miss Mabel M., (1892,) C.
Schenck, Mrs. Mary A., (1892,) C., T.
Senseny, Mrs. Jane, (1838,) P.
Senseny, Miss Jean L., (1886,) P.
Senseny, Mrs. Rose M., (1866,) P.
Sharpe, Mrs. Emma L., (1889,) P.*
Sharpe, Joshua W., (1889,) C., T.
Sharpe, Mrs. Sara F., (1889,) C., T.
Sheller, Daniel M., (1893,) P.
Sheller, Mrs. Jennie, (1893,) C.
Shively, Mrs. McElroy, (1840,) P.
Shumaker, Mrs. Ellen S., (1887,) P.
Shumaker, Frederick H., (1893,) P.
Shumaker, Mrs. Henrietta M., (1893,) C.
Shumaker, Miss Elizabeth C., (1893,) C.
Shuman, Mrs. Estella H., (1888,) P.
Smarsch, Charles F., (1887,) P.
Smarsch, Mrs. Jennie H., (1886,) P.
Smith, Miss Emma L., (1861,) P., T.
Smith, Mrs. M. M., (1868,) C.
Snider, Miss Emma M., (1876,) P.
Snider, Miss Mary M., (1863,) P.
Spessard, Harvey W., (1892,) P., T.
Spessard, Mrs. Sue W., (1892,) C., T.
Stevens, Miss Elizabeth G., (1891,) P.
Stewart, Miss Anna W., (1881,) P., T.
Stewart, Miss Elizabeth K., (1888,) P.
Stewart, Mrs. Jane L., (1863,) P.
Stewart, Miss Janet H., (1893,) P.
Stewart, John, (1876,) P.
Stewart, Miss Mary L., (1887,) P.
Stryke, Miss Sarah A., (1893,) C.
Sudler, Miss Martha V., (1892,) P.
Thompson, Miss Susan A., (1892,) P.
Wallace, Elijah, (1893,) P.

*Died, May 13, 1895.

Wallace, Mrs. Emma M., (1889,) C.
Wallace, Mrs. Mary, (1852,) C.
Wallace, Miss M. Elizabeth, (1866,) C.
Wallace, Thomas H., (1889,) C., Lib.
Wallace, Thomas McI., (1873,) C.
Washington, Mrs. M. C., (1861,) P., T.
Watson, James C., (1892,) P.
Watson, Miss Marian, (1848,) P.
Watson, Miss Martha, (1852,) P.
Werdebaugh, Miss Margaret S., (1891,) P.
White, Mrs. Elizabeth B., (1861,) P.
White, J. Burns, (1871,) P.
White, Miss Jane L., (1893,) P.
Whiteman, Mrs. Annie C., (1892,) C.
Wiestling, Edward B., (1892,) C.
Wiestling, Mrs. Jennie W., (1876,) P.
Wiestling, John G., (1893,) P.
Williams, Robert S., (1892,) P.
Wingert, Jacob F., (1894,) P.
Witherspoon, Andrew H., (1887,) C.
Witherspoon, D. Carothers, (1877,) P.
Witherspoon, Miss Emma, (1887,) C.
Witherspoon, John E., (1887,) C.
Witherspoon, John W., (1874,) C.
Witherspoon, John W., Jr., (1893,) P.
Witherspoon, Mrs. Mary E., (1875,) C.
Witherspoon, Mrs. Mary H. C., (1888,) C.
Witherspoon, Mrs. Rebecca M., (1869,) C., T.
Witherspoon, Mrs. Sarah J., (1872,) C.
Wolverton, Simon P., (1892,) P.
Work, Miss Mary E., (1850,) P.
Wright, Mrs. Matilda, (1893,) C.

The following persons have been received between Nov. 12, 1894, and June 13, 1895.

William Cyrus Hambright, P., Dec. 9, 1894.

William Augustus Culbertson, P., Dec. 9, 1894.
*George Cline Rapp, P., Feb. 14, 1895.
George D. McIlvaine, C., Mch. 2, 1895.
Mrs. Sarah S. McIlvaine, C., Mch. 2, 1895.
John Keasey Britton, P., June 2, 1895.
Mrs. Mede Davis Britton, C., June 2, 1895.
Bruce Elder, R., June 2, 1895.
Henry Guimond, P., June 3, 1895.
Mrs. Kate Senseny McKnight, C., June 12, 1895.

SUPPLEMENTARY LIST.

(See Page 168.)

1838.—Mrs. Jane Senseny, P.—1.
1840.—Mrs. McElroy Shively, P.—1.
1842.—Mrs. Emma L. Sharpe, P.—1.
1843.—William G. Reed, P.; Mrs. Ellen K. Culbertson, P.; Mrs. Rebecca L. Reed, P.—3.
1845.—Andrew M. Criswell, P.—1.
1846.—Mrs. Emeline K. Chambers, P.—1.
1848.—Mrs. Margaret T. Beatty, P.; Miss Mary King, P.; Miss Marian Watson, P.—3.
1849.—Mrs. Catharine Lindsay, C.—1.
1850.—Mrs. Ellen McLellan, C.; Mrs. Abigail McE. Chambers, P.; Miss Mary E. Work, P.—3.
1852.—Miss Louisa Douglas, C.; Mrs. Mary Wallace, C.; Mrs. Elizabeth Huber, C.; Mrs. Ariana R. Kennedy, P.; Miss Martha Watson, P.—5.
1853.—Mrs. Anna M. Clark, C.—1.
1854.—John L. Grier, P.; Mrs. Ellen Chambers, P.; Thomas B. Kennedy, P.—3.
1855.—Mrs. Lucy S. Housum, C.—1.

*Died, Mch. 10, 1895.

1856.—William H. McDowell, C.—1.
1857.—Miss Mary F. Grier, P.—1.
1858.—Miss Kate W. Hayman, P.; Mrs. Lucy C. George, P.—2.
1859.—Mrs. Louisa W. Kennedy, C.; Miss Mary P. Bard, P.—2.
1860.—Mrs. Sarah Andrews, C.—1.

MEMBERSHIP APRIL 1 OF EACH YEAR,

As stated in the Church Register, or as reported in the Minutes of the General Assembly, beginning with 1822, the first year reported.

	Prof.	Cert.	Total.		Prof.	Cert.	Total.
1822,	—	—	106	1840,	8	3	—
1823,	4	1	—	1841,	18	3	—
1824,	3	1	—	1842,	3	6	—
1825,	11	4	110	1843,	6	4	—
1826,	8	3	112	1844,	37	9	130
1827,	7	6	114	1845,	14	2	132
1828,	1	4	114	1846,	5	9	144
1829,	5	3	114	1847,	3	6	144
1830,	1	3	114	1848,	13	5	148
1831,	6	7	114	1849,	5	3	170
1832,	5	9	120	1850,	5	7	170
1833,	11	3	120	1851,	14	6	170
1834,	17	2	120	1852,	3	11	193
1835,	—	1	—	1853,	10	13	188
1836,	3	2	120	1854,	19	5	200
1837,	5	2	120	1855,	3	7	202
1838,	2	—	120	1856,	5	7	210
1839,	4	3	120	1857,	—	9	211

	Prof.	Cert.	Total.		Prof.	Cert.	Total.
1858,	4	11	217	1877,	7	5	306
1859,	18	3	217	1878,	3	3	272
1860,	6	8	216	1879,	5	4	277
1861,	40	13	259	1880,	6	8	273
1862,	10	10	276	1881,	2	3	276
1863,	9	4	284	1882,	5	3	268
1864,	7	12	290	1883,	4	13	270
1865,	3	6	267	1884,	6	11	267
1866,	9	4	254	1885,	15	6	240
1867,	36	19	295	1886,	2	4	242
1868,	3	13	260	1887,	13	5	232
1869,	4	16	244	1888,	29	8	250
1870,	5	8	250	1889,	6	4	246
1871,	10	7	261	1890,	13	8	257
1872,	13	12	280	1891,	26	18	283
1873,	7	2	285	1892,	11	3	274
1874,	1	12	235	1893,	18	13	284
1875,	7	9	243	1894,	39	7	313
1876,	59	2	302				

Membership, April 1, 1822, ... 106
Received by profession, April 1, 1822 to April 1, 1894, 725
    "   " letter, ... - 466

                                                1,297

THE BAPTIZED MEMBERS OF THE CHURCH,

and their Relations to 'the Church.

The Confession of Faith, Chapter xxv, Section 2: "The visible Church . . . . consists of all those throughout the world, that profess the true religion, together with their children." (1 Cor. 1:2; 12:12-13; Gen. 17:7-10; 1 Cor. 7:14;

Acts 2:38–39; Rom. 11:16; Gal. 3:7, 9, 14; Rom. 4:1–25.)

The Confession of Faith, xxviii, 4: "The infants of one or both believing parents are to be baptized." (Gen. 17, 7–10 with Gal. 3:9–14; Rom. 4:11, 12; Acts 2:38–39; Acts 16: 14, 15, 33; 1 Cor. 7:14; Mark 10:13–16.)

Larger Catechism, Question 166: "Infants descending from parents, either both or but one of them, professing faith in Christ, and obedience to Him, are, in that respect, within the covenant, and are to be baptized." (See references above. Baptism in the New Testament Church takes the place of circumcision in the Old Testament Church, and as in the latter infants were circumcised, so in the former infants are baptized.)

I. The Relation of Baptized Children to the Church.

Book of Discipline, Chapter I, Section 5: "All Children born within the pale of the visible Church are members of the Church, are to be baptized, are under the care of the Church, and subject to its government and discipline; and when they have arrived at years of discretion, they are bound to perform all the duties of Church members."

Directory for Worship, Ch. X, Sec. 2: "The years of discretion, in young Christians, cannot be precisely fixed. This must be left to the prudence of the eldership. The officers of the Church are the judges of the qualifications of those to be admitted to sealing ordinances; and of the time when it is proper to admit young Christians to them."

Book of Discipline, XII, 114: "The names of the baptized children of a parent seeking dismission to another Church, shall, if such children are members of his household and remove with him and are not themselves communicants, be included in the certificate of dismission."

II. The Duty of the Christian Parent to the Baptized Child.

Dir. for Worship, VIII, 1, 2, 5, 4: "Baptism is not to be unnecessarily delayed; nor to be administered, in any case, by a private person; but by a minister of Christ, called to be the steward of the mysteries of God. It is usually to be administered in the church, in the presence of the congregation. Although it is proper that baptism be administered in the presence of the congregation: yet there may be cases when it will be expedient to administer this ordinance in private houses; of which the minister is to be the judge. It is required of the parents, that they teach the child to read the Word of God; that they instruct it in the principles of our holy religion, as contained in the Scriptures of the Old and New Testament; an excellent summary of which we have in the Confession of Faith of this Church, and in the Larger and Shorter Catechisms of the Westminster Assembly, which are to be recommended to them, as adopted by this Church, for their direction and assistance, in the discharge of this important duty; that they pray with and for it; that they set an example of piety and godliness before it, and endeavor, by all the means of God's appointment, to bring up their child in the nurture and admonition of the Lord."

Digest 802, 3: Parents should "cause their children to be brought up in the faith of their fathers. We do not mean by this that our youth should be prevented from following out their honest convictions of duty; but that they should be dissuaded from uniting with other denominations from mere caprice or childish fancies. We consider the conduct of those parents who suffer their children to abandon our own Church without any adequate reason, as in a high degree reprehensible, and calculated to inflict a serious injury both on the Church and on their divided households."

6: The placing of children in Romish schools by Protestant parents, is "deemed highly injudicious, fraught with great danger to their children, and utterly inconsistent with every principle of Protestantism . . . . . such conduct in

Church members, whose children have been dedicated to God in baptism, is a violation of their vows made in that ordinance, and a great hindrance to the training up of their children in the nurture and admonition of the Lord."

4: "The institution of Sabbath Schools does not exonerate ministers and parents from the duty of teaching the Shorter Catechism to the children of the Church."

5: "Christian training at all periods of youth, and by all practicable methods, especially by parents at home, by teachers in institutions of learning, and by pastors through catechetical and Bible classes, is binding upon the Church, according to the injunction, Train up a child in the way he should go, and has a vital connection with the increase of the numbers and efficiency of the ministry and of the stability and purity of the Church."

Digest, 834, 3: Parents and others are most earnestly reminded "of the duty of catechising children and youth, and this duty is enjoined upon them, as one whose performance no instruction that children receive in the Sabbath School or elsewhere, outside the family, can supersede or supply."

Digest, 847, 7: "The attention of the whole Church is specially directed to this momentous subject of the duty of home training, in the full assurance that no part of the work of the Church is more fundamental and important than that which is performed in the quietness and sanctity of homes where Christian parents are the divinely chosen and responsible guardians, guides, examples, and teachers of their children, in the way of the Lord; . . . . . . and the utmost diligence is desired in this work; that a generation of God's people, renewed in heart in their infancy, may grow up in the practice of God's worship and service from their earliest years, so that his Church may be more intelligent, zealous, holy and progressive than in any former age."

Directory for Worship, xvi, 1, 3, 4, 5: "Besides the public worship in congregations, it is the indispensible duty of each person, alone, in secret; and of every family, by itself, in private, to pray to, and worship God. Family worship, which ought to be performed by every family, ordinarily morning and evening, consists in prayer, reading the Scriptures, and singing praises. The head of the family, who is to lead in this service, ought to be careful that all the members of his household duly attend; and that none withdraw themselves unnecessarily from any part of family worship; and that all refrain from their common business, while the Scriptures are read, and gravely attend to the same, no less than when prayer or praise is offered up. Let the heads of families be careful to instruct their children and servants in the principles of religion. Every proper opportunity ought to be embraced for such instruction. But we are of opinion, that the Sabbath evenings, after public worship, should be sacredly preserved for this purpose. Therefore we highly disapprove of paying unnecessary private visits on the Lord's day; admitting strangers into the families, except when necessity or charity requires it; or any other practices, whatever plausible pretences may be offered in their favor, if they interfere with the above important and necessary duty."

Digest, 832, 1: "Let heads of families be careful to instruct their children and those committed to their care in the great principles of our holy religion. Let their morning and evening sacrifices be daily offered up in their families to God."

"Parents, train your children in the 'nurture and admonition of the Lord;' your houses should be temples of the living God, in which should ascend to His mercy-seat the continual incense of your daily sacrifices. Pious parents can most effectually preach to the hearts of their children by their affectionate precepts, and their holy example. Your instructions will best prepare them to receive benefit from the public ordinances of religion. And oh! can you see these dearest portions of yourself ready to perish, without earnestly reaching forth a hand to pluck them as brands from the burnings?"

"We have observed with pain, that in some Presbyteries the duties of family religion, and of catechetical instruction, are neglected. Truly it is shameful in men, who call themselves by the name of Christ, not to honor Him before their families, by worshipping Him statedly. Every head of a family is responsible for all its members to God and his country. How can he expect to fulfill his duty, if he does not pray for and with them, and instruct them in the Word of God? If he does not honor God, it cannot be expected his family will. And a Christian family living without family religion is a contradiction. It argues, on the part of such professors, an awful declension and a criminal dereliction of duty."

III. The Church's Duty to her Baptized Children, and theirs to the Church.

Directory for Worship, X, 1, 2: "Children, born within the pale of the visible Church, and dedicated to God in baptism, are under the inspection and government of the Church; and are to be taught to read and repeat the Catechism, the Apostles' Creed, and the Lord's Prayer. They are to be taught to pray, to abhor sin, to fear God, and to obey the Lord Jesus Christ. And, when they come to years of discretion, if they be free from scandal, appear sober and steady, and to have sufficient knowledge to discern the Lord's body, they ought to be informed it is their duty and their privilege to come to the Lord's Supper." (For Section 2, see page 184, above.)

Digest, 801, h: "It is feared that there is a lamentable deficiency in respect to the care and instruction of the baptized children of the Church. Let us, as we value that covenant which makes the promise not only ours but our children's, take a more diligent oversight of these youthful members of our Church. Too often are they left to wander unrestrained and forgotten in the paths of error and of sin. Can the Church answer to her great Head, if this neglect of duty be not mourned over and corrected?"

(See also, as to the duties of churches and ministers, above, pages 168–172.)

THE ROLL OF BAPTIZED MEMBERS.

NOV. 12, 1894.

(Errors in this list or omissions therefrom should be reported to the Pastor.)

Alexander, James Patterson; Alexander, Margaret Scott.

Blair, Mary Stewart; Boyd, Mary Fulton; Boyd, Katie Hillis; Boyd, Joseph Fulton; Brandt, Nellie Pauline; Brewer, John Rowe; Buchanan, Maria Clark.

Chambers, Benjamin Bright; Clark, Andrew Mitchell; Craig, Mary Watson; Crawford, Haslet Wylie; Criswell, John Renfrew; Culbertson, Samuel Duncan; Curriden, Eva Jeannette.

Daniels, Irvin Franklin; Daniels, William Hayes; Davison, John Andrew; Duncan, Calvin Mark; Duncan, Robert Spencer; Duncan, John McClurg.

Edmondson, Eva May; Edmondson, Helen Isabel; Edmondson, Mary Blanche; Elder, Bruce Humbird; Elder, Nellie Grace; Elder, Pauline; Elliott, Robert Hiteshew; Elliott, Anna Margaret.

Fields, John Rufus; Fields, Charles Hunter.

Gehr, Hastings; George, Joseph Chambers; Gillespie, Franklin Stewart; Gilmore, James Ross; Gilmore, William

Blair; Greenewalt, Frank Lindsay; Greenewalt, Margaret Sharpe.

Hambright, Harry Jackson; Hambright, John Stockton; Hambright, Grover Cleveland; Hambright, Ebbert Leroy; Hall, Eleanor Swan; Hibben, Elizabeth Grier; Hoke, Earle; Hoke, Ralph; Hoke, Walter Bruce; Hoopes, Helen.

Kennedy, John Stewart; Kennedy, Moorehead Cowell; Kennedy, Thomas B., Jr.; Kennedy, Thomas B., 3d; Kennedy, James Coyle; Kennedy, Mary Louise; Kennedy, Stewart; Kennedy, William Moorhead; Kennedy, Frank Ulrich.

Langdon, Claude A.; Lesher, Frank Brewer; Lindsay, Frank; Ludwig, Ethyl.

Maclay, Charles Templeton; Maclay, Joseph Pomeroy; Maclay, David Crawford; McDowell, Jane; McDowell, John Clendenin; McDowell, Milton Grier; McDowell, George Davidson; McGowan, William Chambers; McIlvaine, John Stauffer, 3d; McKnight, Joseph; McKnight, Edgar Senseny; McKnight, Arthur Leighton; McKnight, Mary Jane; McLanahan, Sydney Smith.

Nelson, Annie; Nelson, Robert Buchanan.

Orr, Nancy Colwell.

Platt, George Fisk, Jr.; Pomeroy, William McLellan; Pomeroy, John Nevin.

Reed, Elizabeth Stickney, Jr.; Reed, Mary Lindsay; Reed, John Lindsay; Ritchey, Maurice; Ritchey, Frances King; Riddle, Edmund Hunter; Riddle, Henry Alexander, Jr.; Riddle, Robert Forrest; Ross, Winnifred Maria; Ross, Jennie Rebecca; Ross, Alice Chambers.

Schenck, Elsie Mercein; Sharpe, Walter King; Shumaker, Jacob Nixon; Shuman, Elmer Kennedy; Smarsch, John Albert.

White, Samuel Eaton; Wiestling, Crawford Washington; Wiestling, Janet Margaret; Witherspoon, Edith Olivia; Witherspoon, Samuel Clapham; Witherspoon, Andrew Carothers; Witherspoon, Robert Hamilton; Witherspoon, Maurice Marlow; Witherspoon, Andrew Culbertson; Witherspoon, Laura Alice; Witherspoon, David Erskine; Witherspoon, Quinn Mickey; Witherspoon, Agnew Crawford; Witherspoon, Lawrence Austin; Witherspoon, Herbert Wayne.

BAPTIZED SINCE NOV. 12, 1894.

Hoke, Henry Reed, Dec. 25, 1894.
Mehaffey, William Chambers, Jan. 24, 1895.
Kennedy, Francis Atkinson, Mch. 2, 1895.
Britton, Margaret, Jan. 9, 1895.
Wiestling, Elizabeth, May 28, 1895.

CLOSING WORDS.

BY THE EDITOR.

In concluding this chapter of our beloved Church's history, it would be ungrateful not to remark the loving care which the Lord hath vouchsafed this "vineyard which His right hand hath planted, and the branch which He made strong for Himself." (Ps. 80:15.) As we behold two flourishing churches occupying the same Presbyterian territory where a single preacher began the work surrounded by a few Christians who must guard themselves, even when at worship, against painted savages, we may truly say, with Jacob, "With my staff I passed over this Jordan, and now I am become two bands!" But our Church structure cannot create or continue church-life. It can only house it, and form a center of influence. "It is a gross delusion," remarks Guizot, "to believe in the sovereign power of political machinery." And the same is true of ecclesiastical machinery. Men, highminded, devoted in heart, hand and purse to the service of Christ and the help of those about them, and "devout women, not a few," can alone make up a Church. Let the children be the glory of the fathers. Let us prove that we are not the degenerate successors of godly and earnest parents.

> "We're the sons of sires that baffled
> Crowned and mitred tyranny;
> They defied the field and scaffold
> For their birthright; so will we."

The past has gone before. Let it be like the stern-lights of vessels in whose wake we follow, to guide us to noble purpose and practice. Let us love the right and do our duty. The world delights in earnestness. Its rewards go to the earnest. In this God and the world are agreed. When we are filled with Christ, our Church will be filled with Christians. A strong Church is one in which every member feels the power of the Divine Spirit in his soul, and daily lives that power; in which every member understands that Jesus Christ and His Church unitedly require active service from the Christian Army. Let this Church and every member thereof be strong in *spiritual* relations to the neighborhood and the town. Only so can each member stand with a good conscience before God. Let each be a divine agent in helping to overcome evil and establish good. Our responsibility,—the greater because of our gifts and privileges,—is to increase the sum of human happiness by decreasing the sum of human misery.

At the same time, let us not live in the past. The battles of to-day cannot be fought and won with the cross-bow and battle-axe of Crusader days. We cannot live even upon the faith of last year. Let the stalwart faith of us Christians of to-day win battles with our modern weapons which shall match those won by our fathers who conquered these wildernesses for Christ. Age is no protection against error. Let our age renew its youth, resting upon the historic faith of the past, and facing the future with confidence unchanging, in the Lord and Head of the Church.

> "Is Christ in us? Be ours the glorious dower
> To show the Saviour shining in our face,
> And thro' our eyes, faith, putting His sweet power
> To help the weak and wayward with His grace.
> Oh let not sin in us those windows dim
> Through which the world might catch some glimpse of Him."